ADD/ADHD
DRUG
FREE

Natural Alternatives
and Practical Exercises
to Help Your Child Focus

Frank Jacobelli and L.A. Watson

Foreword by Dr. Jay Carter

AMACOM

American Management Association

New York • Atlanta • Brussels • Chicago • Mexico City
San Francisco • Shanghai • Tokyo • Toronto • Washington, D.C.

This publication is designed to provide accurate and authoritative information in regard to the subject matter covered. It is sold with the understanding that the publisher is not engaged in rendering legal, accounting, or other professional service. If legal advice or other expert assistance is required, the services of a competent professional person should be sought.

Although this book does not always specifically identify trademarked names, AMACOM uses them for editorial purposes only, with no intention of trademark violation. The advice concerning drug treatment options is believed to be accurate. However, neither the authors nor the publisher can accept legal responsibility for possible errors in or adverse consequences from the use of these drugs. It is the responsibility of practitioners to check the packaging information as well as to confirm information with the manufacturer.

Library of Congress Cataloging-in-Publication Data

Jacobelli, Frank.
    ADD/ADHD drug free : natural alternatives and practical exercises to
help your child focus / by Frank Jacobelli and L.A. Watson ; foreword by Jay Carter.
        p.   cm.
    Includes bibliographical references and index.
    ISBN 978-0-8144-0094-4
    1. Attention-deficit hyperactivity disorder.   2. Frontal lobes--Problems,
exercises, etc.   I. Watson, L.A.   II. Title.

RJ506.H9J326 2007
618.92′8589—dc22

                                                        2008020767

PRINTING NUMBER

10 9 8 7 6 5 4 3 2 1

Note to the Reader

No book, including this one, can replace the services of a qualified health professional. Please use this book to teach your child to improve his or her behavior, and to help you in communicating with your child's doctor and/or mental health professional so you and your child can obtain the best care possible. If you suspect your child's behavior or thought process is a danger to him/herself or someone else, seek medical attention for your child without delay.

"The creators of *ADD/ADHD Drug Free* pledge our activities to be simple, versatile, crisp, helpful, professional, clever, adaptable, affordable, inventive, and unique."

Frank Jacobelli, MSW, LCSW
L.A. Watson, BA

For Joseph Rosati and John Madison,
who worked so hard to make so much possible.

Acknowledgments

A special thanks to Dr. Jay Carter for his mentorship and for believing in this book from the very beginning.

We will forever hold a special place in our hearts for Sherrill Chidiac, our former literary agent, who taught us the ropes and whose untimely death was a reminder to appreciate everything precious in our lives.

Thanks to Stan Wakefield for his astounding ability to make good things happen.

To Barry Richardson and Andy Ambraziejus at AMACOM for their professionalism.

And to Barbara Chernow and her staff for their patience, guidance, and gifted editorial services. Barbara, you are like a tornado that somehow manages to set everything down in just the right spot.

Lastly, and most importantly, thanks to all the kids who were our teachers.

Contents

Foreword

I would like to personally welcome you to this fine book, a state of the art, practical guide on developing the brain. I respect great scientific information . . . but I want to know how to USE this information, and that's why I am so excited about this book. It is USABLE, and it fills a great need.

I first met Frank Jacobelli at my seminar on bipolar illness. The punch line of the seminar is how the executive functions in the prefrontal lobe go out like a light bulb when a bipolar person is manic. That explains how a normally brilliant person with a lot of common sense can surprisingly gamble away their life savings during a manic episode. They don't see the bigger picture or consequences of their actions. Mania temporarily creates a chemical imbalance similar to taking amphetamines, which blocks the prefrontal lobe and speeds up the cognitive area. So they are thinking faster, but seeing a smaller picture. Without benefit of the prefrontal lobe, their judgment is poor and their behavior is risk laden.

Attention deficit is different as far as the chemical imbalance, but the outcome may be similar in that a person with attention deficit may not see the bigger picture or consequences of their actions. Whether manic or attention deficit, there is very little activity in the prefrontal lobe as shown by Single-photon emission computed tomography.

Normally, one of the significant stages of the development of our prefrontal lobes happens in adolescence. The adolescent begins to develop PERSPECTIVE and becomes SELF-AWARE. (When this happens, the IQs of the parents drop about 40 points, and the parents don't get any "smarter" until this kid has children of his own and realizes that maybe Mom and Dad weren't so dumb after all).

The prefrontal lobe is that part of yourself that SEES what you are thinking and decides whether you are going to say it or not. Preadolescents don't have this ability, in general. If they are thinking it, you are hearing it. The prefrontal lobe is that part of yourself that SEES what you are feeling and decides whether to express that emotion or not. If a child is feeling it, you are seeing what they are feeling. They lack PERSPECTIVE. For the most part, children don't "see themselves" and they are not particularly aware of their surroundings. A child may be standing in front of a door that 50 people want to go through and that child may be oblivious until someone finally says, "Hey! Get out of the way!" We grown-ups tend to find ourselves becoming annoyed with our kids because of this . . . but they just don't have the capability yet.

This capability should be developing, though, and we can help it develop by beating the child, criticizing him, and punishing him. I'm kidding! Actually, human beings have tried all that already, and it doesn't work. Seriously, we can help the children develop the ability to see themselves SITUATIONALLY by using all the excellent tools gathered and presented in this book.

After finally gaining the use of his prefrontal lobe, one child said, "It was like I was nearsighted, and then someone gave me glasses and I could see far." The child was trying to say that he could finally see the big picture of things.

So what can this book do for your child? It can train your child to see the bigger picture so they can envision the goal and, therefore, not give up so quickly, so they don't do inappropriate things, so they don't say inappropriate things, so others don't think they are rude, so they can study knowing the context of what they are studying, so that they don't develop poor self esteem from thinking they are stupid, so they don't think of themselves as a loser because of behavior problems. It can train your child to be empathetic so they can "read" other people, so they can understand others, so they can relate to others, so they can develop tact, so they can have good friends, so they can communicate effectively, so they can eventually have good marriages, so they can teach their own children to use the prefrontal lobe. It can train your child to learn from their mistakes so they don't repeat them over and over again.

I can't tell you how overjoyed I am about this book and I am awed by the excellent job the authors did in putting it together. This book has been a long time coming, with great effort and dedication from the authors, and it is liable to become the "bible" for training and educating children with attention deficit.

This book is the saving grace for the brilliant, albeit reluctant mind, and I thank the authors for bringing it to the kids who will benefit. And you will too.

Dr. Jay Carter

CHAPTER 1

When Medication Isn't the Answer or Isn't Enough

This book was written to give valuable information to parents, teachers, and counselors. But, first and foremost, it is an activity book written for you, the "helper," to use with kids from ages nine to thirteen. The activities are designed to "exercise" their *frontal lobes* and reduce behavior problems associated with Attention Deficit/Hyperactivity Disorder (ADHD) and other frontal lobe deficits. *ADD/ADHD Drug Free* shows you how to impart important skills to kids who need to deal with troubling behavioral and cognitive traits that are most likely biological in nature.

Let's get the elephant out of the room right from the get-go, and begin by telling you what we're *not* and what this book is *not*. We are not scientists, and this is not a scientific book. That's not to say that we haven't studied some of the most recent and most fascinating books and research articles about the brain and how it functions. We have studied those books, particularly the ones about the area of our brain called the *frontal lobes* and about what problems can occur when this part of our brain isn't working up to its potential (more about the frontal lobes later). In fact, you can find references to these works throughout the text, and the titles of these books and articles in the references at the back of this book. These works contain amazing cutting-edge stuff written by people such as Elkhonon Goldberg, Joseph LeDoux, Bruce Perry, Daniel Amen, and Russell Barkley. Now, these folks are scientists! Their books make for fascinating reading for those interested in the science, and we highly recommend them. But we're not experts on the brain or, for that matter, on the neurobiology of ADHD (we'll compare and contrast the types of ADHD in a later chapter). To limit redundancy for now, please note that when we write ADHD, we are referring to all types, whether the problem is primarily inattention, hyperactivity, or both.

As such, we have no double-blind studies with which to convince you of our ideas, but we make no apologies. Science, after all, is very concrete and therefore can sometimes be limiting. If you're looking for "evidenced-based" books on treating the symptoms of ADHD, you're likely to find some, but they will probably be difficult to read and understand. And it's very unlikely that you will find any activity book at all. A practical, enjoyable, hands-on, and effective workbook for kids is long overdue. We are pleased to deliver such a book to you here.

Having gotten that out of the way, we want you to know we're very excited to have this chance to tell you what's worked for the kids we have met—and why. But first, let us tell you what we *are* and a bit more about the book. We are a Mental Health Clinician (Frank) and a Special Educator (Lynn Ann) with more than 40 years combined experience on the front lines in classrooms and counseling offices, providing direct services to kids with frontal lobe problems. Individually, and together, we have treated and taught hundreds of kids who've been pinned with a variety of unflattering labels, such as lazy, angry, crazy, difficult, uncooperative, "bouncing off the walls," or just plain "slow." Over the course of treating all those kids for all those years, we began to notice a few things, and we began to try a few new ideas to address those things we noticed. And what happened was amazing. This book is about sharing our ideas with you: the parents, counselors, and teachers of kids with ADHD and other frontal lobe problems.

But let's back up for a minute. We've known for a long time that kids don't all learn the same way. The funny thing is, despite the truth of it, we (meaning most all well-meaning adults) insist on teaching kids in the same way. We insist on *talking at them* and putting things in front of them to read. This method of teaching may have some real benefit for kids who are good at processing language, but what about the kids who aren't? These are often the kids who won't pay attention, don't follow our rules, may be "bouncing off the walls," or just plain don't get it! What about these kids with less than perfect frontal lobe function? Well, we can tell you that these kids most definitely do not learn best through language (the learning style referred to as *verbal-linguistic*) (Armstrong, 1993). When it comes to "teaching" kids about behaving, dealing with anger, managing emotions (however we want to refer to it), we mostly *tell* them how to behave, what not to do, and, our personal least-favorite, *what to feel.*

Well, one of the first things to dawn on Frank (and we're going back more years than he wishes to count) was that some of the kids he saw in counseling made progress at a snail's pace, while others seemed to blossom before his eyes. Most, particularly those with trouble learning in school, getting along, managing their anger, and completing tasks, didn't seem to take away much from the counseling session. Frank would sometimes watch the child leave his office, feeling a little discouraged in his work. Thank goodness for those others, the one's who were "smart" enough to listen attentively to his eloquence and even feed something back to him from the previous session, perhaps about some coping skill that he had recommended. After being told that it had worked like a charm, he could sit back self-assuredly and revel in the fact that he still "had it!" But deep down, Frank didn't believe that it was about "smarts." And, furthermore, a technique that he considered right on the money (for example, one where the child was asked to look at a page of faces and discuss with him how that person might be feeling) might work great with one kid who was having trouble anticipating the actions of others, but the same intervention with another kid with the same problem might result in the kid looking at Frank as if to say, "you want me to do what, and what was the name of that planet you're from again?"

What *was* going on here? After all, didn't Frank offer his highly skilled clinical ear and life-altering insights to all these kids the same way? It was past time for an ego check. How self-absorbed could he have been? Could it be that Frank had been imparting knowledge, providing choices, and offering support in the manner in which *he* was most comfortable, without any consideration for how his clients might learn best? Were the kids who were progressing in counseling doing so because they happened to be strong *verbal-linguistic* learners like he was? Had Frank neglected to pay attention to how the majority of these troubled kids learn best? Had he neglected the kids who learned best *hands-on* (*bodily-kinesthetic* learners)? And the ones who loved to solve puzzles and try experiments (*logical-mathematical* learners)? There are seven learning styles in all (Gardner, 1983; Armstrong, 1993).

Ouch!

It was about that time that Frank met his coauthor, L.A. Watson, a highly skilled, thoroughly experienced Special Educator and about the most creative, solution-focused individual Frank had ever met. Many, many conversations followed. Frank learned that individual learning styles had been getting attention for several years (Gardner, 1983; Armstrong, 1993; Lazear, 1994) in the field of Special Education and that the more progressive programs were applying this information to "Special Education kids" with learning and behavior problems. Lynn Ann understood early in life (herself a strong *visual-spatial* learner) how a student could become distracted from the *words* of a high-school French teacher because of the teacher's unusual mannerisms and style of dress. Some 30 years later, Lynn can recall almost no conversational French, but she will forever remember (and be capable of drawing) a striking caricature of her eccentric French teacher, including high-heeled shoes, vibrant tight-fitted dresses, red nails, and lipstick.

So, how widely was this information about learning styles being applied to kids with behavior problems? How many special educators were applying it, let alone regular classroom teachers? What about counselors and other mental health professionals? And, maybe the most important question of all, were parents paying attention to how their kids learned best? Was anyone communicating the importance of learning styles to parents?

Where was the *workbook* for ADHD kids and other kids with frontal lobe deficits so they could learn about feelings, getting along with others, and dealing with anger? We couldn't find it, and so we came up with one, an evolved form of which you are now reading. The *coup de grace* occurred when our completed, but yet unpublished, workbook came to the attention of best-selling author, Dr. Jay Carter. Dr. Jay confirmed the need for such a book and the absence of anything like it. We are indebted to Dr. Jay for his tweaking of our thinking, for his invaluable and insightful contributions to this text and, most importantly, for his sincere belief that this workbook will make a real difference in the lives of kids.

Why Yet Another Book About ADHD?

The "brain exercises" (found in Appendix II) are a compilation of all the structured intervention the authors have used with kids over the years. Some worked, and others did not. We believe the ones that worked did so for two important reasons. The first reason, we just discussed: The interventions were presented in the *learning style* best suited to the particular child. Drawing from the previously mentioned example, the *visual-spatial learner* could look at the page of faces, engage in a productive discussion about body language, and then anticipate the actions of others.

The second reason is that the interventions in these exercises served to *jump-start* a part of our kids' brains recognized as being the brain's orchestra leader, battlefield general, or air-traffic controller. The frontal lobes (Figure 1-1) allow us to anticipate the consequences of our actions, anticipate the actions of others, manage our impulses, and see ourselves "situationally."

Situational awareness allows you, the reader, at this very moment, to be aware of where you are and what is going on around you while you read this page. You are aware that you *are* reading this page. You are most likely aware of about how much time you have to devote to reading this book today, and when you must put it down so as to meet other demands in your schedule. And you are most likely aware of the potential consequences of not meeting those demands. Who will be affected? Who might be disappointed? What might happen to the security of your job, or the welfare of your family? *You are aware.* As a matter of fact, you are aware that you are aware. If this sounds like you, then congratulations! Seems as though your frontal lobes are purring like kittens.

Now imagine having a brain with dysfunctional frontal lobes. Imagine being a child with little or no situational awareness. If Billy were

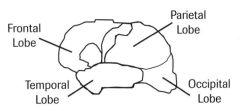

Figure 1-1. Lobes of the brain

giving you a hard time in class, why think twice about reaching across the aisle and giving him a good smack? Would it occur to you ahead of time that the teacher will not only notice, but will also send a note home to his parents for the third time this week? Would you think twice about the undeniable fact that Billy is 20 pounds heavier than you, and he's known for handing out black eyes? Not without situational awareness you wouldn't. Sound like anyone you know? We're betting the answer is yes, otherwise you'd likely be reading the new Grisham book right now instead.

We believe that the frontal lobes can become fit, or at least fitter, through "brain exercise" in much the same way pumping iron builds the muscles of the body. The neurobiologists study the brain's limited ability to regenerate, build new connections, and adapt, and call it "brain plasticity," "vascularization," and "synaptogenesis" (Amen, 2002; Ledoux, 2002; Gold, Reeves, Graziano, and Gross, 1999; Hamm, Temple, O'Dell, Pike, and Lyeth, 1996). We are practitioners, not neuroscientists, and we don't claim expertise in the intricacies of the latest neurological research. *We* believe it, just because it makes sense on a practical level. That is what we have discovered in our work, and that's what this workbook is about.

The brain exercises in this book are specific to kids with behavior problems related to ADHD, and they are organized according to learning style. But don't rely solely on these brain exercises for teaching the kids you're helping to exercise their brains. You will likely find it necessary to drag these kids over to their frontal lobes so often that *their brains will hurt!* (We included that last idea in our first draft of this book and when our agent read it, she immediately phoned us and said to us, "I'm not sure you want to say that their kids' brains will hurt. They might think this book is going to cause a stroke or an aneurysm or something." Well, if you're reading this now, then it means our agent decided to let us leave it in. And if she did, it's a fair bet that the following explanation was enough to satisfy her.)

Can you remember ever taking a college class in statistics? How about learning the computer before the days of Windows? How about taking a foreign language class during the summer session, the one where you get immersed in the language for three hours a day, four days a week? Did your brain hurt? Probably! You were asking things of your frontal lobes that they were just not used to giving. And we're betting that at some point during that adventure, you weren't sure your brain could rise to the occasion. Well that's the kind of *hurt* your kids are likely to experience as you ask them to repeatedly exercise their frontal lobes. Exercise hurts . . . but in a good way. And the exercises, unlike learning statistics, are fun! And it's a good thing.

If the exercises weren't fun for kids with ADHD, their attempts to concentrate on the exercise would actually cause the frontal lobes to under-perform (Amen, 2001). Surely, you've observed your ADHD kids become less attentive and more distractible when asked to concentrate on any task they don't happen to find particularly interesting or novel. The same is true if they are feeling pressured to perform a task. It's important, therefore, that your attitude in working with them on the exercises is patient, supportive, and rewarding (more on this in a later chapter).

Games, such as checkers, chess, and battleship, are excellent ways to supplement this workbook by dragging kids to their frontal lobes, as are some of the old-standard computer games, such as Oregon Trail and Mine Field. Martial arts, taught by a good instructor, is another wonderful way for kids with frontal lobe problems to learn to anticipate the actions of others, to learn cause and effect, and to think situationally (all frontal lobe functions). "Brain Age," a videogame developed by Japanese neuroscientist Dr. Ryuta Kawashima, may prove to be on the cutting edge of game technology that can improve frontal lobe function in kids.

Now a word about the title of this book: Why did we decide to call it *ADD/ADHD Drug Free?* Because we have something we believe is important to offer, and we wanted your attention. Let's clear the air once again. We have seen hundreds of kids "saved" by medications, such as Ritalin, Cylert, Adderall, and Strattera, prescribed by competent physicians in the treatment of ADHD. We've also seen hundreds of kids go without medication and continue to struggle because their parents declined the physicians' advice. Another large group of kids began medications and stopped because of intolerable side effects. Still another significant number continued taking their medication with little or no positive reduction in symptoms. Within this last group, most were receiving counseling as well. A few were even receiving individual and family counseling, and Special Education services. Why, then, were these kids' lives not significantly improved? Well, we'll leave the neurobiology to the scientists, but we know a thing or two about learning styles, and we know about exercising the frontal lobes. We know what's worked.

So, if you think we're suggesting that medication for ADHD is never a good thing, then we've not made this introduction clear (in which case, it may be that our own frontal lobes are due for a tune up). If we've conveyed to you that our work has taught us that the frontal lobes in ADHD kids can be exercised to improve behavior and make for happier kids and that often medication is beneficial and sometimes it isn't, and if we've conveyed that in all cases there needs to be a plan for the child that includes exercising the brain's air-traffic controller, then our introduction is a success, and apparently these old frontal lobes still have what it takes!

Finally, we realize that not everyone will have the time or the inclination to read the entire book. Perhaps you're not interested in what the experts have to say about the brain or ADHD, or how the two are related. Perhaps you would just as soon skip ahead to the activities in Appendix II and start using them with your kids. If this sounds like you, we suggest you have a look at the table of contents and scan the chapter titles for the ones that interest you most. If you elect to get right to the activities, we strongly encourage you to at least have a look at Chapter 8 beforehand. Chapter 8 is a short and to-the-point description of how to make the most of the activities with your kids.

For the rest of you, let's talk kids in Chapter 2.

2

The "Challenging" Child

The labeling of children doesn't come naturally to us, mainly because we strongly believe in the individuality of each child. Each child's individual learning strengths are important, certainly, but learning strengths are just one area of individuality that needs to be recognized and appreciated.

Let's take the highly energetic child for example. This is the little guy or gal who just loves to explore and has a hard time paying attention to any one thing for very long. This exuberant child might be excited by everything from the circular, spinning rack at the dress shop in the mall, to a lone insect that's found its way to the child's classroom desktop. What will determine whether or not this child is labeled ADHD? If given this label, what is it that differentiates the child from other intense, highly energetic, or stressed kids who are not diagnosed with ADHD? And while we're at it, what good does it do to label a child anyway? Let's address the last question first.

We believe the sole usefulness of labeling (or diagnosing) a child is in the hope that doing so will improve our ability to help the child learn, develop, and relate to others in a happy and healthy way. After all, a diagnosis is nothing more that a label placed on the child, based on a group of observable or otherwise verifiable behaviors or other types of symptoms, which may or may not be biologically based (a brain problem). If we know from experience that a child who has that particular grouping of symptoms responds positively to certain kinds of treatment or interventions, then the diagnosis can be used to the child's advantage.

Whether a child's behaviors qualify for a diagnosis, we've learned the importance of taking the time to understand the child as an individual, rather than as a cluster of symptoms that conveniently results in a nice, neat diagnosis. Let's spend a little time discussing the child whose symptoms and problems might not precisely land the child in a tidy diagnostic category.

Not Diagnosable? Then What?

There is a grab bag of labels for these kids, and they include "difficult," "angry," "lazy," "crazy," "slow," "obstinate," "odd," "overly aggressive," and "socially inept." Because the child doesn't fit neatly into a diagnostic category, the helpers (parents, teachers, and counselors) in his life probably struggle with how to actually help. After all, if a child is ADHD he can be given medication. If he's Oppositional Defiant he likely needs long-term therapy (and so might his parents). But what can be done for the undiagnosed child who may otherwise fall through the cracks? Certainly, there's not a one-size-fits-all answer to the question, but we'll tell you what we've learned about these kids.

Henry
Fourth-grader Henry decides to burst out with a couple of juicy obscenities just before lunch and storm out of the classroom into the hallway. In a flash, the labeling process has begun. Because Henry acted out in anger, is he a "bad kid" or a "bully" or is he ADHD and frustrated because he can't concentrate well enough on his work to keep up with his class? Or could it be something else? This is a critical moment for Henry, and he's likely not to be much of an advocate for himself. Why not? Because he's a kid, and kids lack the fully developed verbal skills (and fully developed brain) required to completely identify and verbalize the source of their frustration. Certainly, some kids are better at these important tasks than others. The most Henry can do is signal that he's in trouble and needs help. It's going to be up to the adults in his life to help him put together the pieces.

Henry's actual problem is that his mom and dad have been arguing a lot lately, mostly over money, since his dad hurt his back and has been relying on a disability check to pay the bills. At the same time, Henry's getting extra pressure to push hard in school so that he won't end up stacking boxes in a warehouse like his father. He's been taking hours to fall asleep at night and wakes up feeling exhausted. To make things even worse, Henry isn't the greatest *verbal-linguistic* learner (more about learning styles in Chapter 5), so he has trouble remembering what his teacher (a good verbal-linguistic learner herself) lectures about in class. Henry winds up missing the notes from the last part of the lecture, the homework assignment, and the instructions for the next subject. And the icing on the cake comes when Shaun, the boy who sits behind Henry, can't help but razz him when he doesn't have his math book out in time, and the teacher gets on Henry for holding up the class. So Henry blows!

Observing Henry's apparently lazy behavior since the beginning of the school year a month prior, his teacher has had enough. She sends Henry off to the principal who earlier that morning was reprimanded by the district superintendent for overspending on books. Lacking patience himself, Henry's principal doesn't take the time to understand Henry's behavior. Instead, he reprimands Henry for causing problems in the classroom and interfering in the education of his classmates who are "there to learn." When finally asked why he lost his temper in class, the befuddled Henry can only respond with "I don't know." His principal demands that Henry stay in the chair over lunch and think about the error of his ways. Henry does, but all he can come up with is that he must be a "bad kid."

In reality, Henry is a stressed-out kid, and the pressures put upon him have exceeded his limited coping skills. He hasn't been sleeping, which surely affects his concentration, and to boot he's a physical, hands-on kind of kid (a bodily-kinesthetic learner) who doesn't learn well by somebody *talking at him* all day long. But in all likelihood, without a thought-out plan for helping Henry, he will repeat the inappropriate behavior and soon be handed an unflattering label and a reputation that will be with him for a very long time. In all likelihood, he himself will begin to believe that his shortcomings are solely his own fault. After all, kids are taught to believe what adults tell them.

Should we assume that Henry's frontal lobes are lazy or underperforming? Is the brain attached to an overly stressed fourth grader named Henry suffering from frontal lobe deficits? Surely, given Thomas Armstrong's (1997) valued opinion that even an ADHD-labeled child has a normal brain and Thom Hartmann's belief that the ADHD brain is not abnormal but simply a "hunter's" brain in a world dominated by "farmers" brains and standing out like a sore thumb, Armstrong and Hartmann would almost certainly answer a resounding "no" (more on the opinions of Armstrong and Hartmann later). And while we totally agree that Henry's overwhelmed 12-year-old brain isn't lazy or defective, it's also obvious his brain's "air-traffic controller" (frontal lobes) are way overworked and pretty close to going out on strike! Furthermore, we know from first-hand experience that Henry's frontal lobe function can be given a big-time boost and rise to the occasion. In fact, given the absence of ADHD "symptoms" outlined later in this chapter, we're convinced that Henry's frontal lobes will be supercharged by the "brain exercising" activities in Appendix II. You might refer to working the exercises with Henry as "adding to his coping skills," "presenting him with options," or "giving him some perspective on things." Whatever you decide to call it, we're sure you'll call it just the ticket.

So, what else can be done for Henry and so many like him? For starters, Henry's teacher or principal could listen to Henry, encourage him to talk about what's bothering him, and help him to make sense of his reactions. They could contact Henry's parents and inform them of what resources might be available to Henry, such as the school counselor or a school-based support group for students dealing with difficult life circumstances. Henry's teacher might help Henry with his ability to concentrate by modifying the classroom or his space in the classroom in some way. And she might introduce the topic of individual learning styles to her students and help them understand that it's okay for students to learn differently, and that one way isn't better than another; just different. She could teach Shaun and the others about the value of being a strong *visual-spatial* learner like Henry, and Shaun might even be more inclined to help Henry with his notes. Especially when he realizes that Henry's natural *visual-spatial* abilities are going to help him excel in geometry a couple of years down the road, and Shaun may very well need Henry's help when the time comes.

Henry's parents will need to be made aware of the stress Henry is under. It's very likely that they have become so preoccupied with trying to deal with their financial issues they've lost sight of the bigger picture. Particularly, the impact their arguing is having on their son. Once made aware, it's possible Henry's parents will decide on a more productive way to deal with their fears and frustration. Ideally, they will join with the principal, counselor, and Henry's teacher to carry out a plan for helping Henry cope and succeed in school.

Henry's story was told to emphasize the danger of labeling kids, and thereby maybe even adding to their problems. We know as well as anyone the time and financial pressures that teachers and school administrators face today. But let's remain sensitive to the individual needs of children. Every child is different, both in their biological makeup and in their life experience, and we best not forget it.

Kids and Trauma

Too many kids are living in stressful situations far more damaging than Henry's. Each year in the United States, about five million children are exposed to some form of traumatic experience, and the most common traumas experienced by children are child abuse and domestic violence (Perry, 1999). The results of exposure to these abhorrent behaviors are staggering.

What makes a child violent is a common topic of speculation among the masses. Bullying, beatings, gang activity, even school shootings continue to be of utmost societal concern. The Virginia Tech massacre that shocked the nation in 2007, in which 32 innocent students and faculty were mercilessly slain, is a glaring example of seemingly unexplainable violence, and further reason to more fully understand its roots. Is violence on television the culprit? Maybe hip-hop lyrics? Or maybe there are just too many guns available to kids.

The famous Bobo doll experiment conducted by Albert Bandura in 1961 was convincing evidence that children imitate the violence they see on television. Bandura had children watch an adult play with a grouping of toys that included an inflatable five-foot-tall doll named Bobo, which the adult would intermittently hit on the head with a rubber mallet. Another group of kids watched an adult who didn't hit the doll while playing with the same kinds of toys. After watching this behavior, each child was placed in another room full of toys including a Bobo doll. The kids that had watched the doll being hit on the head with the mallet imitated the violent behavior, while the other kids did not. But violence isn't learned only from television.

In 2004, we had the pleasure of attending a day-long lecture by Dr. Bruce Perry, director of the Child Trauma Academy and an internationally recognized authority on brain development and children in crisis, in Minden, Nevada. But what do brain development and crisis in the lives of children have in common? Plenty, according to Dr. Perry, and he happens to be one of those rare scientists with the gift of making the science almost understandable for nonscientists. We learned from Dr. Perry that the brain of a child who is exposed to traumatic events develops differently than that of a child who is not. Perry confirmed for us that traumatic stress during childhood creates violent, remorseful children. The traumatic experiences cause the "reptilian" (brainstem), less evolved part of the brain, to function abnormally, while in these same children, the highest evolved parts of the brain, such as the frontal lobes (responsible for resisting the impulses of the dysregulated brainstem), are poorly organized because of the chaotic and under socialized development. "This experience-based imbalance predisposes to a host of neuropsychiatric problems and violent behavior" (2007).

Despite these recent and invaluable revelations, Perry warns, "as we search for solutions to the plagues of violence in our society, it will be imperative that we avoid the False God of Simple Solutions. The neurobiology of complex, heterogeneous behaviors is complex and heterogeneous. In the end, paying attention to neurobiological impact of developmental experiences—traumatic or nurturing—will yield great insight for prevention and therapeutic interventions." We wholeheartedly agree, and we can't emphasize strongly enough the importance of a safe, nurturing, and peaceful environment for every child to exercise his or her birthright to reach full potential as a human being.

In homes where violence isn't a problem, there may still be a lack of support and guidance. If we want these kids to have the kind of skills taught in this book, somebody's going to have to teach them. Is it reasonable to hold a child accountable if they've never been taught? We think not.

Temperament

Another critical factor in the mind's ability to regulate emotion, and therefore behavior, is that of temperament. Temperament is commonly thought to be an intangible. A child may be shy or precocious, reserved or boisterous, delicate or rough and ready. And who's to say what determines which it will be? The term itself, temperament, seems a layperson's, without any real scientific basis at all.

We were given food for thought by psychologist, lecturer, and best-selling author, Dr. Jay Carter, while attending his Sacramento lecture on anger management in 2000. Dr. Jay, as he's frequently called, was discussing temperament in children and the need for a therapist to consider the individual child's temperament in working with the child to solve problems, particularly of the interpersonal variety.

Dr. Jay gave his audience the example of the golden retriever and the pit bull. If a golden retriever puppy is battered and abused as a puppy, it's likely to be fearful, skittish, and shy away from people. But a pit bull battered and abused as a puppy is quite likely to behave in the opposite manner. The pit bull will likely be aggressive and easily provoked into action. Temperament, Dr. Jay noted, is something a child is born with. Simply put, the experiences of the child will react with the child's individual temperament to determine the child's behavior. When trying to help a child with their behavior problems, it's worth noting whether you're dealing with a pit bull or a golden retriever.

Daniel Siegel, child and adolescent psychiatrist and UCLA professor, takes the concept of temperament to another level. He attributes temperament, which he too acknowledges varies widely from individual to individual, to the rich and complex circuitry of the brain, which is the result of both genetic factors and events that may occur during pregnancy. Siegel writes, "Temperament describes some of the aspects of inborn characteristics, including sensitivity to the environment, intensity of emotional response, baseline global mood, regularity of biological cycles, and attraction to or withdrawal from novel situations" (1999). It seems, no matter how you slice it, the brain is involved in every aspect of who we are.

There are numerous diagnoses given to kids with behavior problems, ranging in severity from Adjustment Disorder to Conduct Disorder. Some, such as Bipolar Disorder, which is often mistaken for ADHD, will most often require the involvement of a child psychiatrist for the purpose of managing medication. When Bipolar Disorder is misdiagnosed as ADHD and stimulant medication is prescribed, the results are often catastrophic. The child might possibly exhibit psychotic symptoms, such as delusions and auditory hallucinations. Other disorders, such as Attachment Disorder, will require highly specialized treatment. A common theme among psychiatric disorders occurring in childhood is the inability to behave in a socially appropriate manner.

For purposes of brevity, we will be discussing only two of the most commonly diagnosed "disorders" that occur in childhood and contribute to behavior problems: Attention Deficit/Hyperactivity Disorder and Oppositional Defiant Disorder, two problems for which the activities in this book can make an invaluable difference.

Attention Deficit/Hyperactivity Disorder (ADHD)

Web sites and magazine articles are often dropping names of famous people from the past who are said to have had Attention Deficit Disorder. Those most frequently referred to include Ben Franklin, Galileo, Thomas Jefferson, Leonardo da Vinci, the Wright Brothers, and Albert Einstein. Two of the more recent additions to the list are Bill Clinton and George W. Bush. No one can argue with the fact that all these people are high achievers, and some unquestionably fall into the "genius" category. This fact hopefully serves to inspire kids and their parents alike. But some may use this as further evidence to question the existence of the "disorder" in the first place.

The DSM-IV-TR, published by the American Psychiatric Association, is currently the mental health clinician's bible for diagnosing psychiatric disorders. According to the DSM, the essential features of attention deficit/hyperactivity disorder include "a persistent pattern of inattention and/or hyperactivity-impulsivity that is more frequently displayed and more severe than is typically observed in individuals at a comparable level of development" (2000). Other criteria must be met before the diagnosis can be made, such as clear evidence of interference in social, academic, or occupational functioning, and some of the symptoms that cause impairment have to be present before the age of seven. The person labeled ADHD often has trouble paying attention to detail and he or she often shifts attention from one uncompleted task to another. Work is often messy and performed without much considered thought. The ADHD-labeled person often has trouble with organization and typically avoids activities that require much mental effort or sustained attention. Activities that are novel and stimulating are far better at holding the attention of the ADHD child than those that are lengthy, monotonous, or repetitive. The authors' gave this fact special consideration in creating the activities in Appendix II.

Hyperactivity is often, but not always, present in the individual labeled ADHD. The person may be fidgety or squirmy and have a hard time staying in their seat, even when leaving their seat would be an infraction of the rules, such as in the classroom. The DSM describes this behavior as if the person is being "driven by a motor."

Impulsivity, also frequently but not always present, may be in the form of impatience, a kind of pressure to speak, act, or react, even when not doing so would be more socially appropriate and lead to fewer unpleasant consequences.

These symptoms can occur in a number of settings, such as school, home, work, and social situations. For the person to be diagnosed with ADHD, there must be impairment in at least two settings.

For more detailed diagnostic information, readers should review the DSM-IV-TR criteria themselves or have a discussion with their child's mental health provider or a qualified pediatrician.

The ADHD Controversy. Is It for Real?

Thomas Armstrong (1997) believes that the ADD diagnosis gained tremendous popularity in the 1990s because it served as a tidy way to explain away the complexities of American society at the close of the twentieth century. He doesn't believe the disorder exists and cites societal factors to explain the behavior and learning problems that "ADD children" experience. Among those factors are the breakdown of the family, the erosion of respect for authority, mass media's creation of a "short-attention-span culture," and stress levels that have skyrocketed. Armstrong writes, "when our children begin to act out under the strain, it's convenient to create a scientific-sounding term to label them with, and a whole program of ADD/ADHD workbooks, videos, and instructional materials to use to fit them in a box that relieves parents and teachers of any worry that it might be due to their own failure (or the failure of the broader culture) to nurture or teach effectively." Armstrong supports the efforts of parents and teachers to recognize the individuality of each child, including their learning strengths, and in addressing their specific needs.

At the opposite end of the spectrum is Daniel Amen (2001), who not only believes that the disorder exists and supports the use of medication to address the symptoms, but also believes he has the pictures to prove it (see Chapter 3). The legions of experts in each of these camps, believers and nonbelievers, are huge. Amen's camp includes the publishers of the DSM-IV-TR (the American Psychiatric Association) and Russell Barkley, whom you might say wrote the book on ADD/ADHD, *Attention Deficit Hyperactivity Disorder*" (1998). But with regard to medication for ADHD kids, Barkley reports that 10 to 20 percent of kids diagnosed with ADHD and started on medication don't show improvement. He adds that of the 70 to 80 percent who do show improvement, some experience side effects severe enough that the medication is discontinued.

Among the nonbelievers in Armstrong's camp is Howard Glasser, Executive Director of the Children's Success Foundation, internationally renowned lecturer, and best-selling author. So strongly does Glasser oppose the idea of labeling intense children and medicating them that he wrote *101 Reasons to Avoid Ritalin Like the Plague* (2005). Among his 100 reasons, Glasser cites reason 20, "Children on Ritalin report being cut off from their feelings," and 27, "Ritalin can cause loss of appetite, weight loss, and stunting of growth in children."

In 2000, more than 19 million prescriptions for ADHD drugs were filled, a 72 percent increase over 1995, representing possibly the most dramatic increase over any previous five-year period. Adding to the controversy, the dramatic increase in their availability has contributed to the abuse of these drugs, which are now considered "street drugs," frequently obtained illegally. A study of students in Wisconsin and Minnesota showed 34 percent of ADHD youth age 11 to 18 reported being approached to sell or trade their stimulant medications, such as Ritalin (Thomas, 2000).

As the controversy rages on, the authors prefer to leave the dispute and the evidence gathering to the scientists and researchers. What we know for sure is that the kids we've worked with who met the diagnostic criteria for ADHD benefited from the brain-exercising activities contained herein, and that's what matters to us. We're convinced it should matter to you.

In 1994, the American Psychiatric Association stopped recognizing Attention Deficit Disorder and Attention Deficit Hyperactivity Disorder as two separate disorders. With the publication of the Diagnostic and Statistical Manual (DSM-IV) in 1994, the combined heading of Attention Deficit/Hyperactivity Disorder remained, and three subtypes were added to better specify the types of symptoms the person is having. There is (1) the Combined Type (314.01) where both significant inattention and hyperactivity/impulsivity are present, (2) the Predominantly Inattentive Type (314.00) where most of the problems are about difficulty paying attention, and (3) the Predominantly Hyperactive Type (314.00) when most of the problems have to do with hyperactivity/impulsivity (American Psychiatric Association, 1994). Subsequently, a "text-revised" edition of DSM-IV (DSM-IV-TR) was published in 2000.

Author Thom Hartmann (2002) refers to the hunter and farmer societies as a fascinating analogy for giving his perspective on ADHD. First there were the hunters, who relied on their alertness, reflexes, mobility, and keen ability to scan and react, to eat and feed their families. Later came the farmers, who stayed put, planted crops in neat, organized rows, and didn't mind the less stimulating and highly repetitive chores that farming required, such as turning the soil, planting, pulling weeds, watering, and harvesting.

The farmers, with their predictable food supply and fixed locations, were highly suited for reproducing and, before long, farmers greatly outnumbered hunters. So, as societies developed, they were designed to accommodate the majority: the farmers. Hartmann considers the ADHD brain to be the brain of the hunter which is highly capable at doing what it was designed for: scanning, moving, and intensely reacting. But the hunter's brain is at odds with much of the farmer society's expectations. The classroom, for example, is organized into nice neat rows, much like the crop field, and the student is expected to stay put and quietly perform repetitive acts. Therefore, those students with farmer brains have a far easier time of it than do those with the hunter brains. Is it fair to conclude that the ADHD brain is working efficiently, just *differently* than the majority of brains in society? If we were expected to roam and hunt for our supper, how would the farmer brain fare, we wonder? How well would the *normal* brain adapt, in comparison to the ADHD brain?

Undoubtedly, children are being either overdiagnosed or under-diagnosed, most likely because of concerns about unnecessarily medicating children who may actually be behaving normally for their age and gender and because of the context-dependent nature of the behaviors associated with the diagnosis. In simpler terms, a child may appear to be hyperactive when sitting unattended at the kitchen table where he is expected to concentrate on his math homework while his younger siblings are playing his favorite videogame in the next room, but he may not appear to be hyperactive while playing on his little league team or acting in the school play. In terms of age and gender considerations, the hyperactive behavior of a normal six-year-old may be greater than the restless or impulsive behavior of a 10-year-old boy, which has earned him a diagnosis of ADHD. Believe in the disorder or not, here are some facts: ADHD accounts for 30 to 40 percent of all referrals made to child guidance clinics, family and primary care physicians, and pediatricians (Connors, 2006), making it one of the most commonly diagnosed mental disorders among children. Several studies reported that two to five percent of school-aged children have well-defined symptoms of ADHD, and boys are three to ten times more likely to carry the diagnosis.

Adding credence to the position of those who view ADHD as an undeniable brain-based disorder, a 2007 study led by neuroscientist Philip Shaw of the National Institute of Mental Health reportedly found a genetic variation that boosts the risk for ADHD. Researchers scanned the brains of 105 children with ADHD and 103 brains of kids ages 8 to 16 without ADHD. They found that parts of the brain's cortex that are important for attention were thinner in the ADHD-afflicted kids. The study went on to conclude that "people who have the risk gene have a distinctive pattern of brain growth that normalizes with age" (Singer, 2007). According to Shaw, it may be that ADHD kids with this particular variant are more likely to grow out of the disorder as their brain matures and grows than are other ADHD kids. Among the other possible genetic factors contributing to risk of the disorder is a variation in a receptor for the neurotransmitter dopamine. This variant is thought to increase risk for ADHD by 20 to 30 percent.

No single cause of ADHD has been identified. A variety of genetic and biological factors give rise to the disorder, the common resulting factor being a disturbance in the frontal cortical-striatal network of the brain (Barkley, 1998). ADHD is not caused by bad parenting. It's nobody's fault! However, early physical and emotional neglect will keep the brain from developing properly, and ADHD symptoms can result. Hereditary factors contributing to ADHD are well documented. A close relative of a person diagnosed with ADHD is five times more likely to have ADHD themselves than will a member of the general population (American Academy of Pediatrics, 2004). The following is a list of possible causes or contributors to ADHD symptoms:

Possible Causes of ADHD or Contributors to ADHD Symptoms
- Genetics. ADHD tends to run in families.
- Biological/Physiological Causes. Brain injury, often unknown to the child or family.
- Brain-chemical problems. The key neurotransmitters associated with mood, emotion, and behavior include dopamine (emotion, thought processing, movement, and reward), norepinephrine (alerting, focusing, orienting, hunger, thirst, emotional reward), and serotonin (mood, depression, anxiety, aggression, violence, carbohydrate craving).
- Complications in pregnancy or childbirth. Particularly those that disrupt oxygen to the fetus.
- Poisoning from lead or other toxins.
- Diet. Allergies to certain foods or imbalances in nutrition.
- Prenatal alcohol or drug exposure.
- Medical problems. Certain medical problems, such as an overactive thyroid can look like ADHD (see Table 2.1).

Oppositional Defiant Disorder (ODD)

All children are oppositional from time to time, particularly when stressed, tired, hungry, or bored. They may talk back, argue, disobey, and

Table 2.1. Some of the conditions other than ADHD that can include attention and organizational problems

Psychiatric conditions	Medical Conditions
Schizophrenia	Head Injury
Bipolar Disorder	Hypo- or Hyperthyroidism
Depression	Renal or Hepatic Insufficiency
Posttraumatic Stress Disorder	Anoxic Encephalopathy
	Vitamin Deficiency

From Barkley, 1990.

defy parents or teachers. In children diagnosed with Oppositional Defiant Disorder (ODD), however, there is an ongoing pattern of defiant and hostile behavior toward adults in authority that significantly interferes with the child's day-to-day functioning.

While a disorder unrelated to ADHD, ODD is presented here because kids diagnosed with either of these disorders often display similar problem behaviors, and the activities in this book have proven effective with kids diagnosed either way. In addition, a child is about twice as likely to be diagnosed with ODD as ADHD. Five to fifteen percent of children and adolescents in the United States meet the criteria for a diagnosis of Oppositional Defiant Disorder, as compared to three to five percent of children diagnosed with ADHD. A child diagnosed with ODD is about three times more likely to be male than female.

The causes of ODD are most likely multidimensional. That is, a number of factors may contribute to the pattern of oppositional defiant behavior. Research supports that the content and rate of stimulation in TV, movies, and videogames contributes to increased behavioral problems. American children watch an average of three to four hours of television per day. More than one hundred studies have shown that kids become immune to the horror of violence and many gradually accept violence as a way to solve problems. Many kids imitate the violence they observe on TV and often identify with certain characters, victims, and victimizers.

A study conducted by the American Academy of Pediatrics concluded in 2001 that the frequency of watching wrestling on TV positively correlated with increased date fighting and with other behaviors that put one's health at risk. The same study concluded that the frequency with which children watch violence on television correlated with kids and adolescents carrying guns and other weapons, nonprescription use of stimulant medication, and driving after drinking.

It should be no surprise that the quality of parenting also directly impacts the behavior of kids. The presence of violence and emotional abuse in the home, even if not aimed directly at the child, correlates with a greater increase of behavioral problems in the child. Additionally, a study by Lehigh University in 2001 concluded that preschool children who receive severe physical discipline are at increased risk of engaging in overly aggressive behavior during their school years.

Overly permissive parenting resulting in a lack of appropriate behavioral expectations is also known to contribute to behavior problems, as does the individual makeup of the child's brain and genetics. How might a child's brain be impacted by the onslaught of technology-driven activities that are superstimulating to the senses (and therefore the brain) such as videogames? And what is the effect of the 24-hour-a-day "real time" coverage readily available today on television, of unfolding events, and detailed and repetitive visual coverage of disasters and violent crimes?

A 20-year study by The Rational Psychology Association in Munich, Germany, looked at the effects of technology on the brain. The study of 4000 subjects every five years yielded some very interesting findings. In 1980, the study found that it was becoming more and more difficult to stimulate the cerebral cortex of the brain. The results indicate that our sensitivity to stimuli is decreasing at a rate of about one percent per year, as delicate sensations are being filtered out and brutal stimuli responded to. The report further concluded that, "as visual stimuli go in, entire areas of the brain are being skipped over, and this optical information is being processed without actually being evaluated" (MEDS-PDN, 2007). This, the study concludes, has a significant impact on emotional response and how the brain is networked. A logical interpretation of these conclusions might be that children are able to watch violent and gruesome videos and television without experiencing emotion and learn to only pay attention if it's extremely exciting and stimulating.

One might conclude that a "new brain" has been developed as a result of the technological boom and the exposure of our children to the overwhelming but ultimately pleasurable stimulation of no-holds-barred television, violent "action" movies, and probably the most stimulating and addictive pastime of all, the videogame. This new brain is likely to have evolved in any one of us born after about 1969. The cerebral cortex, dulled-down by this "mind numbing" stimulation, is likely a brain unsatisfied by what those of us born prior to 1969 would consider enjoyable stimulation. And the child attached to such a brain is likely in search of greater and greater levels of stimulation, almost certainly contributing to behavioral problems.

According to the DSM-IV-TR, the essential feature of Oppositional Defiant Disorder is "a recurrent pattern of negativistic, defiant, disobedient, and hostile behavior toward authority figures that persists for at least six months" (2000). Other criteria need to be met for a diagnosis of ODD to be made, such as defying or refusing to comply with the rules of adults, deliberately doing things that annoy other people, blaming others, or being vindictive. The child labeled ODD is often stubborn and argumentative and frequently tests limits set by adults. Once again, the reader interested in more detailed information on how a diagnosis of ODD is made should have a look at the DSM or talk with their child's pediatrician or mental health professional.

Whether helping a child labeled ADHD, ODD, difficult, angry, slow, or socially inept, the activities contained in Appendix II have successfully reduced the symptoms and behavior problems in the hundreds of children the authors have taught and counseled. We are confident they will do the same for your child.

CHAPTER 3

Your Child's *Amazing* Brain

Boiled-Down Neurology for
Nonscientists . . . by Nonscientists

Normal, a Myth?

Astounding advances in brain imaging technology over the past 20 years have proven that the vast majority of brains are imperfect. In fact, according to Daniel Amen (2001), a psychiatrist and pioneer in the use of Single-Photon Emission Computed Tomography (SPECT) which explores how brain function relates to behavior, only about one in 25 brains is perfectly normal. An abnormal brain could be caused by a number of factors. Genetics (ADHD runs in families), head injury, exposure to toxins, medical problems, drug abuse, and even physical and emotional neglect can cause or contribute to brain abnormalities, including ADHD. That's the bad news.

Thankfully, there's good news. Until relatively recently, brain experts believed that the brain you were born with is the brain you're stuck with. Not so. Of late, a common buzzword in the field of neurology is *neural-plasticity*, or just plain *plasticity*. The term refers to the ability of neurons to change the way they behave and relate to one another as the brain adapts to the environment (Cozolino, 2002; Golden, 1994).

Does this mean that spending quality time with your kids and coaching them through the activities in this book will change their brains, specifically, the part of the brain most associated with ADHD, the frontal cortex, for the better? The brain's CEO? Its air traffic controller? No one can say for sure. Or at least, no one can prove it "scientifically." But make no mistake; the human brain is an organ of adaptation to the physical and social worlds. The quality and nature of relationships are translated into codes within neural networks that are the core ingredients of the brain and the mind. Through these relationship and learning experiences, nature and nurture become one (Cozolino, 2002).

Samuel and the Amygdala-Prefrontal Cortex Connection

Samuel is an 11-year-old fifth grader, labeled ADHD, who's really into sports. At recess, Samuel is chosen last when teams are being picked for soccer, and he's horrified. His heart begins to pound, and the muscles in his jaw tighten. Nearly immobilized by his emotional reaction, Samuel is slow to join his team. His team captain remarks that Samuel is wasting recess time, and Samuel blows. What has just occurred in Samuel's brain?

Neuroscientists tell us that the emotional center of the brain is the amygdala, an almond-shaped structure deep in the area of the brain called the limbic system. The amygdala is hard at work as Samuel's emotional intensity and impulsivity is set off by his perception that he isn't as good an athlete as his peers and that his classmates don't particularly value his athletic ability. This is a major blow to a young boy who lives and breathes sports. At the same time that the amygdala begins to fire, another part of the brain is activated. The neocortex located in the frontal lobes, just behind the forehead, acts as a damper switch to the amygdala. Its function is to allow for a more reasonable and appropriate response to the perceived insult or injustice (Goleman, 1995). In Samuel's case, his neocortex isn't up to par because of his frontal lobe deficits and is no match for his fully functioning amygdala.

Antonio Damasio, neurologist and author of *Descartes' Error,* carefully studied patients with damage to this prefrontal-amygdala circuit. He found that their decision making was often disastrous, despite no deterioration in IQ or any cognitive ability. He concludes that their decisions are so bad because their ability to temper emotion with reason is limited by the imbalance in the functioning of the amygdala and prefrontal cortex (1994).

The amygdala plays an important role in a person's survival, as well as the survival of the species. It gives us a quick, emotional take on what's happening around us and pushes us toward action important for our survival. The amygdala plays a key role in our (and our ancestors') split-second decisions to escape or attack, to eat, or to reproduce. It's the prefrontal cortex that gives us a better thought out plan for dealing with the situation at hand, however. Its proper function is essential in allowing us to delay our impulses if it makes sense to do so, to see the big picture, and to proceed in a rational way that is appropriate within our societal context.

Elkehon Goldberg, Clinical Professor of Neurology and author of *The Executive Brain: Frontal Lobes and the Civilized Mind,* writes, "The frontal cortex plays the central role in forming goals and objectives and then in devising a plan of action required to attain these goals. It selects the cognitive skills required to implement the plans, coordinates these skills, and applies them in correct order. Finally, the prefrontal cortex is responsible for evaluating our actions as success or failure relative to our intentions" (2001).

The Tragic Story of Phineas Gage

To better understand the relationship between the prefrontal cortex and aspects of personality and behavior, it may be useful to tell the story of Phineas Gage. In 1848, at 25 years of age, Gage worked as a construction foreman for the Rutland & Burlington Railroad in Vermont. Gage was five-foot-six and athletic. He was reportedly precise in his movements and light on his feet. In addition to his physical gifts, the aspiring railroad man was loved by his crew and highly valued by his employers, who described him as the most "efficient and capable" man in their employ (Harlow, 1868).

A common duty performed by Gage and his men was the blasting away of rock. The process involved, first, drilling a hole into the rock then filling the hole about half way with blasting powder. Next, Gage would insert a fuse and cover the powder with sand. Finally, the sand would be "tamped in" or compacted with a careful sequence of strokes from an iron rod, three-feet long, an inch-and-a-quarter around, and weighing a hefty 13 pounds. If all went well, the sand would prevent the blast from being delivered outward and direct it into the rock beneath.

At 4:30 on a particularly hot afternoon, Gage is said to have inserted the fuse and instructed a worker to add the sand. Distracted momentarily by a question from another worker, Gage was confused and began pounding the powder with the tamping rod, without the sand having been layered on top of the powder. Well, you might guess what happened next. A stroke from the tamping rod caused a spark, and the powder was ignited. The blast had a different and far more intense sound than the usual blasting away of the rock and included was an odd whistling sound, as of a missile being delivered skyward. The workcrew froze in a moment of disorientation, no one quite sure as to what had just occurred. What had indeed occurred was a direct assault on Gage by the iron bar, which had entered his left cheek, pierced the base of his skull, obliterated the front of his brain, and exited at a high rate of speed through the top of his head. Gage fell to the ground, stunned, but awake. The rod eventually landed about a hundred feet away.

The accident made all the local papers, and readers were stunned that Gage had survived. By one account, Gage's men helped him into a cart and delivered him to the nearby road, where he got out of the cart under his own power. Within an hour of the explosion, Gage met with the local doctor and described the circumstances of the accident in detail, his skull protruding outward around a two-inch hole and his brain visibly pulsating inside. Incredibly, the doctor later described Gage's account of the accident as "perfectly rational."

Phineas Gage was determined by his doctors to be healed in a matter of only two months, but his doctors couldn't have predicted what was to become of young Phineas. So different had his disposition become in the months and days that followed that his friends commented, "Gage was no longer Gage." He was now "fitful, irreverent, indulging at times in the grossest profanity which was not previously his custom, manifesting but little deference for his fellows, impatient of restraint or advice, when it conflicts with his desires . . . devising many plans of future operation, which are no sooner arranged that they are abandoned."

Not allowed to return to his job because of his new personality, Gage took jobs on horse farms. Apparently prone to throwing tantrums, Gage was let go from several farm jobs before going to work for Barnum's Museum in New York as a circus attraction, where he would display his wounds along with the tamping iron that caused them.

Four years after the accident, Gage abruptly left for South America where he worked driving a stagecoach in Santiago, Chile. He later returned to the United States and moved in with his mother in San

Francisco. Still, he had no ability to keep a job. By 1860, Gage's health had deteriorated and he began to suffer epileptic seizures. On May 21, he suffered a series of convulsions from which he never regained consciousness. Phineas Gage was buried in San Francisco; the tamping iron that shattered not only his skull, but his promising life, was buried with him.

The sad story of Phineas Gage is worth telling because his tragedy shed light on the purpose and function of the part of the brain which, historically, scientists have known least about; namely the area destroyed in the accident: the frontal lobes. Gage's drastic behavior change was convincing evidence for many that social behavior, including planning, maintaining attention, and managing impulses, required a particular region of the brain. In those early days of neurological research, such an idea was far more unthinkable than the belief that there could be a specific brain region responsible for movement, language, taste, or vision. In summary, the story of Phineas Gage hinted at a previously unknown and amazing fact: There are systems in the human brain "dedicated more to reasoning than to anything else, and in particular to the personal and social dimensions of reasoning" (Damasio, 1994).

Improved Fitness for Young Frontal Lobes

Scientists tell us that psychotherapy is effective because it causes microscopic changes in the structure and, therefore, the function of the brain (Siegel, in Cozolino, 2002). However, the most common model of modern psychotherapy, namely cognitive behavioral therapy, has been shown to have little if any positive effect with ADHD kids, even when a child is also taking the most effective ADHD medications. This is not surprising, because successful cognitive-behavioral therapy requires the client to be able to take a hard look at what behaviors have been working and which haven't. In a nutshell, to be successful the client needs some ability to focus on what kinds of thoughts he or she has been having about a particular life circumstance, explore other ways to think about the problem, recall what he or she has tried to do to fix it, and decide whether the outcome was the desired one. If it wasn't, the client will need to choose a different behavioral option, and repeat the process.

Considering the importance of the prefrontal cortex in all of these steps, it's no wonder cognitive behavioral therapy tends to get ADHD kids (and their counselors) nowhere.

Yet, *certain aspects* of cognitive behavioral therapy *do* show positive results with ADHD kids and their families (Barkley, 1998). Activities that teach "cognitive restructuring," that is, learning to think differently about a problem, "rehearsing," that is practicing anticipating difficult situations, and "self-regulating," such as paying attention to keeping breathing and heart rate under control, have been shown to be beneficial. And activities that serve to improve parent-child relationships have resulted in improved functioning and a decrease in symptoms of ADHD. Elements of these skills are taught in the activities in Appendix II, and more.

Could this be why the activities contained in this book have been remarkably successful in helping kids reduce their symptoms of ADHD? Could the positive effects of coaching time with your kids, with special attention to the particular learning strengths of your child, geared toward thinking, feeling, and behavior, actually change the structure of your child's brain for the better? Well, we know what's worked for our kids, and we believe these activities will work for yours. Furthermore, the experts tell us that it's not only psychotherapy, but also "cognitive exercise" that can strengthen the frontal lobes of the brain (Goldberg, 2001). The authors are soundly convinced that the brain-training "exercise" contained in this book is responsible for strengthened brains in the hundreds of kids we've taught and counseled, resulting in decreased symptoms of ADHD.

It should be noted that many of the kids labeled with hyperactivity that we have taught and counseled were taking appropriate stimulant medication, prescribed and monitored by their pediatrician or neurologist. In most instances, those who were taking the medication learned better, both in the classroom and in the counseling office, than those kids who weren't on medication. The majority of kids who weren't taking medication, either because their parents were against the idea or the kids couldn't handle the side effects, improved through the use of the activities contained in this book, just not as much as the kids taking the medication. In our opinion, and in the opinion of Daniel Amen, the right stimulant medication for the particular child changes the brain in these kids for the better (Amen, 2001).

However, not every child labeled ADHD exhibits such severe learning and behavioral problems that make rushing them to a doctor for medication a no-brainer, particularly in light of the controversy surrounding the overmedicating of kids and the potential harm that stimulant medications can cause. The authors completely respect the right of parents to research the issue independently, consult with their child's physician, and make the informed decision they feel is in their child's best interest.

That having been said, ADHD kids tend to have excessively slow brainwave activity in their frontal lobes, which worsens when they try to concentrate (Lubar, 2004; Amen, 2001; Barkley, 1998). Stimulant medication, such as Ritalin, Dexedrine, or Concerta, may serve to stimulate the brainwave activity, having a calming effect on the child, and improving his or her ability to concentrate (Amen, 2001). Neurotherapy, also referred to as neurofeedback training, has also shown promise in lessening ADHD symptoms by helping to normalize the ratio of theta (slow) to beta (fast) brainwaves (Lubar, 2003).

We recognize the ongoing controversy about the possible overprescribing of medications for kids suspected of having ADHD with predominant hyperactivity-impulsivity. One particular "expert" on the subject once said to me, in all sincerity, "ADHD is nothing more than a label given to kids who are more active than someone else wants them to be." It may be worth noting that for a number of our kids, particularly those with only marginal learning and behavioral problems linked to ADHD, following a brief medication trial with no clear improvement, the medication was discontinued by the doctor and the child was no worse for wear. Following such a medication trial, the child's parents were generally satisfied that they'd at least given the medication a try, and they went on to help their children using nonmedical means.

And so as the controversy rages on with no foreseeable end in sight, let us remind you of the importance of treating each child as an individual. Keep in mind the possibility of emotional, social, or nutritional reasons for inattention and/or impulsivity, as well as other "symptoms" or behavioral problems.

In summary, we will say it again here: If you suspect your child has ADHD (particularly with inattentiveness and hyperactivity), get him or her to a competent pediatrician or neurologist for assessment without delay. And if medication is recommended, we suggest that you don't dismiss the idea out of hand. Ask the doctor about the potential benefits and risks associated with these medications, and do some research on your own. If you choose to begin your child on medication and he or she is able to tolerate the possible side effects, your child will likely be better able to pay attention, plan ahead, organize, be less irritable, and better able to anticipate consequences. Once in that improved state of mind, using the activities contained here should help your child dramatically improve his or her behavior. That is our sincere belief. That is our sincere wish for you and your child.

The Brain's Air-traffic Controller

A piece of brain tissue the size of a grain of sand contains about 100,000 neurons and about a billion synapses (huge numbers on a scale difficult to imagine). A neuron is simply a nerve cell located in the brain. What makes neurons unique, though, is that they can communicate with one another in a way that other cells in the body cannot. Synapses are the small gaps between the neurons. The electrical impulse travels down the neuron and, before reaching the end of the nerve fiber, causes the release of a chemical called a neurotransmitter. The neurotransmitter moves across the synaptic space and attaches to the dendrite of the next neuron, thereby completing its mission by closing the gap. This process of neural and synaptic transmission is in play with everything the brain does (LeDoux, 2002).

The brain experts tell us that the part of the brain most closely associated with ADHD is the prefrontal cortex (PFC), the region of Phineas Gage's brain obliterated by the tamping rod. The PFC is the surface area of the frontal lobes located directly behind the forehead. This is the part of the brain that gives us "situational awareness." It supervises and coordinates our behavior. It is the seat of the brain's "executive" functioning. If our PFC isn't working properly, we're likely to have trouble controlling impulses, paying attention, planning, organizing, or anticipating the consequences of our actions.

The prefrontal cortex is made up of three sections, the dorsal lateral section, (which is on the outside surface of the PFC), the inferior orbital section (on the front underside of the brain), and the anterior cingulate gyrus (which runs through the middle of the prefrontal cortex, or between the lobes, if you will. Daniel Amen, in *Healing ADD* (2001), claims to have identified six different types of ADHD using the SPECT scan. Although all six types of ADHD are at least partially attributed to a problem in the frontal lobes, at least two of the six involve other structures of the brain, such as the temporal lobe and the limbic system. The temporal lobe is involved with aggression, among other things. The limbic system is involved in mood, particularly depression, gloominess, or sullenness. Therefore if one of those regions of the brain is contributing to the ADHD, your child may exhibit corresponding symptoms.

The PFC, the last part of the brain to evolve, makes up about a third of the entire brain. In chimpanzees, the PFC makes up about 12 percent of the brain, 7 percent of a dog's brain, and only 3 percent of a cat's. Could this be why you're likely to see more squashed cats in the road than dogs or . . . chimpanzees? Okay, maybe there are other reasons, such as a cat's ability to scale a six-foot fence without breaking a sweat, but you get the point.

Plenty of well-functioning prefrontal cortices make for a brain attached to a boy or girl likely to be calm, organized, able, and willing to follow direction (most of the time) and to possess a built-in ability to predict what's going to happen next if he or she were to reach over and give that ornery classmate a good smack.

The learning and behavior problems associated with ADHD are caused by subtle dysfunction of the frontal lobes and the pathways connecting them to other parts of the brain (Goldberg, 2001; Hallowell and Ratey, 1995). In fact, because the frontal lobes were the last part of the brain to develop in what are now referred to as "modern humans," one might say that *not* having ADHD is a condition that has arisen relatively recently in the process of evolution. One might just imagine the ADHD "symptoms" present in pre-modern humans who had little or no frontal lobes at all.

An Ancient Historical Perspective

Today's society is chock-full of distractions in comparison to, let's say, the time of the Homo heidelbergensis premodern humans, some 500,000 years ago. During that period it was necessary to hunt, gather, and reproduce. Not much more was expected nor was more necessary to maintain the lifestyle of the time. There were no specific schedules to keep, bills to get in the mail, and voicemails and e-mails to respond to. It wasn't necessary to obey traffic laws while getting one child to soccer practice and delivering the second to dance class across town. So how important were frontal lobes anyway? The heidelbergensis, after all, weren't bombarded with advertising, traffic, homework, or retirement planning. And multitasking wouldn't truly become an issue for another half-million years or so.

Surely, our ancestors of the period were faced with important challenges, such as remembering to stay clear of the stomping ground of the biggest, baddest man-eating beasts and adapting to changing environmental conditions, such as drought and inclement weather. And unformed frontal lobes may explain why these premodern humans rarely lived beyond their twenties (to their credit, the Homo heidelbergensis may have been the first humans to bury their dead, and anthropologists tell us they may have also been first to take a crack at tool making).

Recent programming on the Discovery Channel, *Rise of Man*, aired on July 5, 2007, explained that over time, the human brain grew in size (much of the gradually added brain is what we today refer to as the frontal lobes) as a result of ancient people's need to observe and study the environment to survive as a species. Included in these early observations was the eventual ability to observe and study the footprints of animals. As a result the hunter was more adept at feeding his family, and at keeping track of the whereabouts of potentially deadly beasts, further supporting the concept that "brain-exercise" enhances frontal lobe development and function.

We hold fast to the belief that today's fast-paced, distraction ridden, "plan ahead or lose out" society makes the need for smooth-running frontal lobes undeniable. Indeed, if our kids were living the lifestyle of their heidelbergensis equivalents, would anyone in their right mind be looking to label them ADHD? We think not.

We'd like to introduce you to some very special children in Chapter 4.

Gabriel, Patrick, Denny, Tad, and Jeremy

A Few of Our Kids

Over the course of our careers, we have worked with hundreds of kids with behavior problems, and many of them were diagnosed with ADHD. Lynn Ann worked as a teacher, special educator, and resource specialist, and Frank as a mental health clinician. For eight of those years, we worked closely together, sharing thoughts, ideas, and strategies in trying to help the troubled children and families of a small and isolated mountain community. The Colorado community in which we worked is difficult to describe to anyone who hasn't been there. The kindergarten-through-eighth-grade school, the community's *only* school, is nestled among the fir trees and ponderosa pines. The community is home to fewer that 2,000 residents, living in clusters on sanctuaries of private land. Much of the surrounding area is a vast reserve of pristine national forest. Almost a third of the residents are Native Americans, and nearly the entire balance is Caucasian. The views are breathtaking, and the locals are certain they've found paradise. Still, there is no bank, hospital, dry cleaners, barbershop, or full-time physician. Lynn Ann is the only Special Educator in the community and Frank is the only Mental Health Clinician for fifty miles. The community has its challenges.

While we've changed the names of the kids and a few facts to preserve the anonymity of the community and the individuals that reside there, we owe a debt of gratitude to each of them, and to their families for all that they taught us. Our lives and our professional skills were made better by knowing them and we're grateful.

You will likely notice that we have elected to write about five boys in this chapter and not a single girl. Throughout the book, we often use the pronoun "he" when referring to a child labeled with ADHD. We want to emphasize that it is not our intent to write a "sexist" book or to imply that ADHD is strictly a "boy problem." While some recent studies have concluded that girls may be grossly "underdiagnosed" in comparison to boys (Swan, 2007) and that girls diagnosed with ADHD are less likely to exhibit the same degree of hyperactivity as boys (Rabiner, 2006), boys continue to be diagnosed at a rate 2 to 9 times higher than girls (APA, 2000). And possibly because the predominant symptom in girls tends to be inattention rather than hyperactivity, they are less likely to cause a fuss that results in a referral to a clinician for diagnosis. As a result, we have identified far fewer girls with ADHD than boys.

Gabriel

Gabriel was a Latino-Native American butterball-of-fire with a crew cut and big dark eyes. His blazing smile could melt ice and in brilliant contrast, depending on his mood, he had a scowl that could make a raging river consider changing direction.

By the time Frank was introduced to Gabriel, he was a seven-year-old second grader. He'd been a special education student since the age of three, and he'd been kicked out of preschool after two days. Seems he had a thing for throwing food, and he'd thrown his bowl of cereal against the wall when his teacher had asked him to take his seat. Immediately following a bout of anger, Gabriel would clam up and sulk for a good long time. Eventually, he'd regroup long enough to participate appropriately for a short time and, then, start the cycle all over again.

Lynn Ann worked closely with Gabriel, doing what she could to teach him simple social skills. Getting him to sit and eat a meal without throwing his food was considered quite an accomplishment, given Gabriel's brief but colorful track record. Lynn Ann administered a widely used ADHD assessment called the Connor's Continuous Performance Task (CPT). Based on the results, she referred Gabriel and his mother to a pediatric neurologist, whose office was a county away, 40 miles through an 8,000-foot mountain pass. The doctor diagnosed

Gabriel with ADHD and began a trial of Ritalin, which Gabriel resisted taking at first. He eventually became used to the idea and showed improvement in his ability to resist his impulses and pay attention. Gabriel was eventually allowed to return to school, but the improvement resulting from the medication alone was far from improvement enough.

Gabriel showed little interest in anything being taught by his teacher, and a mere suggestion that he stay in his seat and pay attention was met with a deaf ear or outright defiance. He was also incredibly sensitive about being touched and aggressive toward anyone coming close to him. Anytime a classmate would come near, Gabriel would lash out in anger by hitting, kicking, or biting.

Gabriel was moved to a special day class, where he had only a handful of classmates and the lights could be lowered to further reduce distracting stimulation. Lynn Ann began by introducing the concept of "personal space" in terms Gabriel and his classmates could understand. He was presented with a length of rope and told that he could make a rope circle on the floor whenever he needed his personal space respected, and the other kids were to stay outside. Gabriel was reassured that if anyone came into his space, he was to let his teacher know. *She* would see that his space was respected. The rope circle was also a visual reminder for Gabriel to not impulsively wander off from his desk or his spot on the floor at times when doing so would be inappropriate. In a matter of days, Gabriel was able to verbalize his need for personal space: *"I need my space right now."* Unlike before, Gabriel could do so without a tantrum and fleeing to a place where he would sulk. *Empowered* by the idea of owning his personal space and reminded by the rope as a *visual* cue, Gabriel quickly began to exert socially appropriate *self-control*. But there was far more to do.

Another strategy was to introduce Gabriel to the computer . . . and it was love at first sight! He proved nimble with his hands and fingers, and he was smitten with the idea of being able to make amazing things happen with just the push of a button or the click of a mouse. Gabriel's confidence began to grow, and his self-esteem along with it.

We worked together to develop a behavioral plan that emphasized proper social skills and improved ability to follow directions. We began with very simple expectations and achievable goals. Gabriel was told that if he were able to stay in his seat, do his work, and be pleasant to others for 15 minutes, he would be allowed to play on the computer for ten minutes. The goal was achievable, and Gabriel was successful. Over time, the expectation was gradually increased. Twenty minutes . . . 30 . . . 45. Gabriel gained confidence by managing his behavior for short periods of time and felt fortified in tackling the longer periods.

Gabriel's mom played an instrumental part in his educational and behavioral plans, and she was consistent in implementing the plans in the home setting as well. He was rewarded with a donated computer of his own to take home, and his computer skills continued to improve. Gabriel finally began to enjoy learning. Furthermore, it quickly became obvious that he particularly enjoyed using his hands and excelled in the *bodily-kinesthetic* style of learning. To further improve his ability to articulate his thoughts (thereby reducing his frustration and emotional reactivity), speech therapy was introduced and quickly proved to be an important component of the overall plan.

Gabriel's individual counseling sessions with Frank consisted of helping him to identify his feelings and use words (rather than acting out) to get his needs met. This proved difficult at first, but became easier as they practiced. Knowing how much Gabriel loved using his hands and how satisfied he felt with his ability to do so, Frank brought blocks into the office for reinforcement. As with the classroom behavior management, a few successful minutes of counseling time was rewarded with a few minutes of playtime.

Frank had a habit of putting his big wad of keys down on his desk in those days, and the temptation proved way too much for Gabriel on more than one occasion. Early on, Frank had been reminded of the distraction as Gabriel would grab the keys in the blink of an eye. Frank would have to figure out how to retrieve them, without bringing on a tantrum, and put them into a drawer. Out of sight, out of mind. Before long, Frank realized that allowing him to hold and flip through the keys was self-soothing for Gabriel, and Frank allowed him to do so as we ventured further and further into uncharted territory: the land of feelings and how to deal with them.

Gabriel was introduced to the concept of noticing his anger in its early stages (see activity: Tom Takes His Temp), and he spent several counseling sessions practicing strategies for staying in control (see activities: Don't Blow It, Mad Me, and Picture This)

To strengthen his interpersonal skills, Gabriel was presented with simple circle drawings of faces, each with one of the five basic feelings: happy, sad, mad, scared, and confused (See activity: I Know That Face). He struggled at first, but he was soon able to correctly identify the facial expression most closely associated with a particular feeling. Next, Gabriel and Frank practiced on each other. Gabriel would make a face, and Frank would guess what feeling he had in mind. If Frank was correct, it would be his turn to make a face. If Gabriel were able to correctly identify all five feelings, you guessed it, 15 minutes on the computer.

While working a booth at a local health fair just a few weeks ago, nearly six years after Gabriel and his family left the community, Frank met up with his mother. Carla is a gentle and soft-spoken Native American woman and is blessed with the same brilliant smile as her son. She informed Frank that Gabriel was about to graduate from high school! He'd been able to stop his Ritalin in the ninth grade, and he planned to attend a technical school to learn welding after graduation. Knowing Gabriel's bodily-kinesthetic abilities, Frank wasn't the least bit surprised at his career choice.

Carla beamed with pride.

What We Learned from Gabriel

It was obvious from day one that Gabriel, like most ADHD-labeled kids, wasn't a strong *verbal-linguistic* learner. You could rant, reprimand, lecture, and stomp your feet till the cows came home, and it wasn't going to make a dent.

Gabriel was the kind of kid who needed to relate to the world tactilely, hence the constant urge to touch everything, including his classmates. By trial and error, we eventually learned how to best relate to Gabriel, first by introducing tactile strategies. The hands-on approach was soothing to Gabriel and, once soothed, he was better able to focus on learning about how to relate to others. Once better able to relate to his peers, teachers, and counselor, and believing he'd earned their respect, Gabriel was then better able to focus on learning academics.

It was necessary to teach Gabriel in the ways he learned best, that is to say, using *his* learning strengths and not only *ours*. We used hands-on board games to teach social skills, the computer to teach math, and storybooks with *movable* parts to teach reading. The results were impressive!

Working with Gabriel was a reminder of the importance of treating each child, no matter what diagnosis or unflattering label they may carry, as an individual. Each child's needs are specific, and even if they share the same diagnosis as another student, that's surely no guarantee that they will learn or relate in the same way.

Gabriel was truly a gift for us in developing our ideas, and we are certain that he has an important gift to someday share with his fellow man.

Denny

Denny was a slim, blond, and highly emotional third-grader when his family moved to town. He would cry at the drop of a hat, usually when frustrated, and he was quickly subject to put-downs by his classmates. Before long, Denny was not only diagnosed as Attention Deficit and Hyperactive, but also down on *himself* and miserably depressed.

It seemed that Denny had no control over himself and he was always in trouble with his teacher. He craved attention and wanted nothing more than to be liked. It was heartbreaking to watch him struggle with rejection on a daily basis. No sooner would he arrive at school than he would inevitably be curled up on the classroom floor, crying over some perceived failure or insult from a classmate. If Denny *wasn't* curled up on the floor, you might find him under his desk or out of his seat and headed for places unknown. He just couldn't keep still!

It didn't help that Denny's classroom was noisier than most, and Denny's teacher allowed the kids to leave their seats pretty much at will. A classmate passing by or, worse yet, brushing Denny as he or she passed was enough to get Denny out of his seat and into trouble. It was as though he was one big hair trigger, and just about any stimulation was enough to get him to commence firing. Denny's classroom environment was a set-up for failure, and Denny's chance of success without serious intervention was nil.

Lynn Ann assisted Denny's classroom teacher in making the room a bit more *Denny friendly*. Ms. Ross was encouraged to add a bit more structure. Rather than allowing the kids to leave their seats at will, they would now be required to ask and could only move about the class for good reason, such as to sharpen a pencil or retrieve supplies from their cubby. The idea was to reduce the overstimulation and add a bit of predictability for all the kids, especially Denny.

Next Lynn Ann put blinders on Denny. Textbooks were stacked on either side of Denny's desk, a good two feet high. The books served to screen out visual distraction and created a safe zone within which he could more effectively concentrate. Denny thought that was *"cool."* This technique was attempted with a number of ADHD-labeled kids over the years, and it wasn't always accepted with enthusiasm. Sometimes a student will feel singled out or picked on when this strategy is implemented. It's a good idea for the teacher to be creative in how the idea is delivered to the child. A lot of boys like the idea of being inside their "fort," a safe and cozy place in which to do their business.

Frank worked individually with Denny on learning to pay attention to his body (see activity: X Marks the Spot). *What does it feel like when you start to wind up? Where do you feel it? What do you notice? What can you do to stop from getting wound tighter and tighter?* These were questions that dragged Denny over to his frontal lobes, and no one had bothered to ask them before. Had it been reasonable to expect Denny to know how to manage his behavior if he'd never been taught?

Denny relished the individual attention of one-on-one counseling, and he beamed for the entire 30 minutes or so. He was willing to try just about any activity Frank suggested and, with a little practice, Denny was soon able to describe the physical sensations that accompanied his behavioral problems in detail (see activity: Mad Me).

"It's like electricity in my bones," he would say, "and butterflies in my stomach." Eventually, Denny boiled the description down to a concise phrase that conveyed to others that he needed help, and right now: "I'm getting fidgety."

It was obvious from day one that Denny was overflowing with excess physical energy, much of which he used to fret, complain, worry, and fidget. He needed a way to burn it off. And so we had an idea on one particularly difficult day, and Denny was taken from class to the track, where he was encouraged to run, which he did gladly. After ten minutes he returned to the classroom a little sweaty and a lot more focused and ready to learn.

Now able to *recognize* he was getting into trouble and *put it into words,* Denny was able and willing to ask to go outside and burn off that troublesome excess energy that accompanied his ADHD. Luckily, the school's track wasn't in total view of any of the classrooms. His teacher could just barely see the top of his head but Denny felt as though he could run in private, and run he did! Paying attention to his body and behavior, Denny got into the habit of asking to run for ten minutes or so, around 11 AM. every day. The exercise made it possible for him to stay in his seat, focus on his work, and feel good about himself at least until after lunch. Without it being suggested by the adults in his life, Denny began running the track at recess, further evidence that the technique made him feel better. On a couple of occasions he got into a little trouble for leaving the classroom to go run without asking first. He was into it!

In counseling sessions, Denny began learning how to take a break from stressful situations that might lead to a meltdown, so that when he really needed to, removing himself from the situation wouldn't feel like such a foreign thing to do (see activity: I'd Rather Walk).

Denny's mom supported the school's attempts to find ways to help Denny manage ADHD, as did the parents of most of the kids whose ADHD symptoms were brought under control. Denny's mom used some of the same interventions at home that were helping in school. We can't emphasize the importance of parent involvement enough.

What We Learned from Denny

Denny had an extreme amount of physical energy to release. Once given a way to vent that energy, he was better able to focus in the classroom. He was a bright student who could handle the academic subjects. Because he didn't have a learning disability, moving Denny to the special education classroom was never seriously considered. Strategies needed to be implemented so that he could calm himself, focus, and learn. Because Denny could himself notice how much better he felt after running, it didn't take long for him to begin asking to leave for a few minutes so that he could run and expel the excess energy. He therefore was able to gain some mastery over the problem and improve his confidence and self-esteem. No longer was he being "told" to leave the classroom and come back "normal." He was *choosing* to use a strategy that he himself knew was helpful.

In working with Denny, we were also reminded of the critical importance of having the cooperation of teachers, parents, and others who were involved with Denny on a daily basis. It was critical that Denny's behavior plan be comprehensive and carried out in all social settings. Because of the buy-in from teachers and family, Denny was keenly aware of the plan's importance and of the positive effect it was having in all areas of his life.

After working with Denny, we began receiving requests to teach our interventions to the academic community, as well as to parents' groups, extended family members, and even probation officers. "It takes a village to raise a child" rang true in Denny's case, as he needed the support of everyone around him.

We were particularly proud of how hard Denny worked to be able to explain what was happening inside him, as the great flood of energy and restlessness would begin to build. Little does he know that, through his effort and determination, he will be indirectly helping many others like himself!

Patrick

Patrick was a freckle-faced fourth grader attending a small private school when his parents first asked Lynn Ann to evaluate him. It turned out to be no easy task. During that initial visit, Patrick engaged in some impressive acrobatics, spinning on his back on the shiny hardwood floor, completing ten or 20 somersaults, and playfully terrorizing the family dog or cat, whichever was unlucky enough to be in Patrick's general vicinity at any given time.

It seemed Patrick was always in trouble and despite his pediatrician's recommendation, Patrick's parents decided not to consider stimulant medication to treat his ADHD. Lynn Ann's mission was to conduct a behavioral/learning analysis, then suggest nonmedical interventions that might make a difference in Patrick's life. Interestingly, Patrick listened to Lynn Ann's every word and could flawlessly repeat what she'd said without missing a beat, while impressing her with acrobatics. This was obviously a bright boy, and it initially seemed to Lynn Ann that his problem wasn't so much attention deficit, but rather hyperactivity without much of an attention problem at all!

Lynn Ann recommended cutting out food additives and sugar from Patrick's diet, consistency in disciplining, and adding structure to his day. She was able to measure Patrick's academic standing and reported to his parents that he hadn't yet fallen behind, but she was extremely concerned about his lack of social skills. Lynn Ann encouraged Patrick's parents to reconsider the doctor's recommendation for medication. Instead, they scheduled their son to see Frank. They were hopeful that counseling, along with the behavioral plan Lynn Ann had suggested, might do the trick.

So hyperactive was Patrick that Frank's first challenge was teaching him to walk from the lobby to his office without detouring. Patrick seemed unable to resist dodging ahead to hide behind a hallway file cabinet or the counseling office couch.

The first few individual sessions consisted of Patrick and Frank playing The Social Skills Game, a structured approach to teaching about appropriate behavior, decision-making, and emotions. It was obvious from the beginning that Patrick could participate in the game with ease, as long as he was allowed to engage in the same or similar gymnastics as those Lynn Ann witnessed in Patrick's home weeks before. But there was a twist. It seemed Patrick couldn't resist the impulse to cheat at nearly every turn!

Impulsivity, hyperactivity, smarts, terrible social skills, and charm. A more rounded picture of Patrick was emerging. Unfortunately, being cooped up in the office, regardless of the structure of The Social Skills Game, wasn't going to cut it. They needed to get out, and get moving.

Frank and Patrick walked and talked among the pines. Patrick was encouraged to talk about his relationships: friends, dad, mom, and teacher. Frank hoped to help Patrick gain some awareness into his social struggles (see activity: This Thing Called ADHD). Possibly Patrick would begin to recognize how his impulsivity and hyperactivity were negatively impacting his life (see activities: Cool Like Who? and Life on the Line). And if so, might he be open to learning to behave more appropriately?

But while walking and talking, Patrick couldn't seem to stay on course. Any interesting object within 20 feet on either side of the trail was simply too much temptation. Tree limbs were turned into swords or spears, pine cones became grenades, trunks of trees made for exciting hiding places, and any therapeutic conversation became a vague memory.

Several weeks passed without progress. It was time for a meeting with Patrick's dad and mom. Frank explained the difficulty in making any therapeutic progress given the extreme degree of Patrick's distractibility and impulsivity. Frank had no choice but to strongly encourage them to reconsider the pediatrician's recommendation. Possibly Patrick's parents would give more credence to a recommendation from a pediatric neurologist. Frank suggested they take Patrick to the doctor.

Mom and dad exchanged a glance and thanked Frank for his time, while rising from their seats. The meaning was obvious. No Ritalin for our son!

Before leaving the office, Patrick's mom told Frank she expected to be busy over the next couple of weeks, so she'd call for Patrick's next appointment. This was a common practice with clients or parents of clients who'd decided not to continue in counseling. Frank tried his best not to feel a sense of relief. Without medication, it seemed any future sessions with Patrick would serve no good purpose.

Two years passed before Frank and Patrick's father happened to meet up at the local post office.

"Gotta tell you, Patrick's doing really good," Patrick's dad began.

Could Patrick have grown out of his ADHD? Then the self-doubt crept in. Had Patrick been seeing a more competent therapist? Someone more sophisticated in behavioral therapy with ADHD kids?

"That's good to hear," Frank replied. A half-truth.

"Yeah, the medication made a world of difference."

Well, there it was. Patrick had responded to Strattera. Still *energetic,* Patrick's hyperactivity had been greatly reduced by the medication. Frank hadn't been Patrick's therapist in years, so he wanted to be careful not to pry or make assumptions. What he wanted to say was, "Well I sure hope Patrick is seeing a good therapist who can help him get caught up on his social skills." But Frank didn't say that. Instead he complimented Patrick's dad on his persistence.

"You didn't give up, and that's really great. Let me know if there's anything more I can do for Patrick," he hinted.

Patrick's dad smiled and nodded, and walked to his car. It seemed he could deal with Patrick either being in counseling or on medication, but not both. Possibly the combination was just too stigmatizing, which is unfortunate. With Patrick's ADHD mostly controlled with medication, we're convinced he'd have done extremely well in counseling, bright as he was.

A year later, Frank was asked by the local school to do a short presentation to the eighth graders on "dealing with anger." While standing and delivering in front of the class, Frank was keenly aware of Patrick as he chatted impulsively with the boy next to him. Fresh-faced and freckled, Patrick was the picture of health and happiness. When Frank asked him to save his socializing for recess, Patrick gave an apologetic nod. It was a good three minutes before he was back chatting with his neighbor again. Patrick was a good kid, respectful and well-meaning. Was his inability to stay focused during the presentation a symptom of his ADHD? Or was it about the years he'd spent overwhelmed by symptoms and the resulting lack of social skills?

What We Learned from Patrick

Patrick was a very smart boy, but he'd fallen way behind in developing social skills. To complicate matters, his peers had accepted, even expected Patrick's gyrations, intrusions, and impulsive acts of all kinds. The stifling of social skills is a common occurrence among ADHD kids, who are sometimes able to excel academically despite their behavior. Many become depressed as they slowly become social outcasts, shunned by their peers. Patrick managed to avoid becoming a social outcast through his charm. We learned a number of things from Patrick.

We learned that there is good reason to teach social skills to people of all ages whose social development has been stifled by ADHD. Not catching up is sure to result in an adult with a multitude of interpersonal problems with coworkers, friends, and family.

We learned that in many cases, certainly in Patrick's case, the right ADHD medication is remarkably beneficial for reducing hyperactivity, thereby making him more open to learning about appropriate behavior. The repetitive practicing of social skills is essential, and a gyrating, spinning, bouncing bundle of energy, acting on every impulse is in no condition to practice. Medication won't *fix* the problem, but in Patrick's case, the medication seemed to make it possible for him to *begin* to catch up. Catching up will be a process for Patrick, and it won't happen overnight.

We also learned that just because a child "appears" to be "actively" engaged in an activity other than the task at hand doesn't mean that he or she isn't listening to every word. We want to thank Patrick for his keen ability to "listen." We imagine him as an adult, gainfully employed as an undercover FBI or CIA agent, "listening" attentively while appearing to be "doing" something completely unrelated. Patrick is truly a talented young man!

Tad

Frank first met Tad when he was four years old and in Head Start. Tad's teacher had asked Frank to observe Tad in class as he interacted with his peers. She was concerned about Tad's low frustration tolerance and his aggressiveness. His teacher had phoned Tad's mom and finally convinced her to allow the local mental health clinician to have a look at Tad.

Frank watched as the crew-cut Native American boy was supposed to be settling in for a nap. Instead, Tad lay face up on the mat, wiggling restlessly and pushing at the kids closest to him with his feet. He whined softly, seemingly feeling imposed upon by his peers. Within a few minutes of observation, Tad's restlessness began to escalate, and it was obvious to Frank that Tad was having a tough time. Tad's teacher called out to Tad to settle down. He responded with an indecipherable shout and more stiff jabs of his foot.

Unwilling to ask Tad to move to a less populated part of the mat, thereby risking a meltdown, Tad's teacher finally intervened by sliding his neighbors an extra few inches away from him. To this, Tad turned on to his belly and began to sob, eventually falling asleep.

Later that afternoon, Frank watched as Tad and his classmates worked at connecting the dots. Every few seconds, Tad would look at the paper of the child next to him, and scowl. This went on for nearly five minutes before the scowl turned to a pout, and Tad threw his pencil across the room, then put his head in his hands and sulked. It seemed that Tad had been comparing his work to the boy's next to him and he hadn't liked the comparison. Having seen this particular behavior pattern before, Tad's teacher was able to redirect him by suggesting he move to a far corner of the room to play with the blocks that were stacked there. Tad let out a grunt and pushed back from the table so violently, that his chair tipped backward and hit the floor with a smack! When Tad moved to the corner of the room, the relief on his teacher's face was obvious.

"We dodged a bullet this time," she told Frank. "Usually there's no breaking the pattern. Once he gets frustrated with himself, he gets angrier and angrier until I have to call his mom to come get him and take him home."

It seemed damage control was the common strategy when Tad was in the classroom. What *power* this little boy commanded.

It was obvious to Frank that Tad was in need of a more thorough learning and mental health assessment. Once the issues could be better understood, then a treatment plan could be put in place. Treatment with a four-year-old always meant involving the parents, maybe even the whole family.

"Tad's mom didn't even want me to call you," his teacher told me. "I don't think she believes in counseling."

It was decided that Tad's teacher would approach his mother and ask that she sign a consent for mental health treatment. This seemed our best shot at getting Tad into treatment, because his teacher and mother were acquainted and on good terms. But she refused, and Frank's phone calls were not returned.

Three years passed. Tad eventually entered treatment after his mother was charged with physically abusing his younger brother, and his brother was removed from the home. At that point, the social worker assigned to the case was able to use some leverage with his mother and write individual counseling for both Tad and his brother, as well as family counseling, into the reunification plan.

Finally able to do an assessment and get a history, Frank learned that Tad's biological father had been abusive and had died in a motor vehicle accident when Tad was four years old. Tad's mom had remarried, and Tad managed to bond with his step dad, but when Tad was six, his stepdad tragically died as well. At seven, Tad's older cousin, while trying to teach Tad about the dangers of playing with matches, carelessly set Tad's polyester shirt on fire, causing a painful burn. An assessment by the pediatric neurologist resulted in a diagnosis of ADHD. In addition, Frank added two more: posttraumatic stress disorder (PTSD) and oppositional defiant disorder. Tad was to be our biggest challenge. (It should be noted that symptoms of PTSD can mimic ADHD. If ADHD is suspected, the parent or evaluator should rule out PTSD before making the ADHD diagnosis. Was the child exposed to a traumatic event? Was the child out of the parents' care, during which time a traumatic event might have occurred?)

By the time Frank was able to meet with Tad in the first grade, Tad was remarkably disruptive in the classroom. The same self-critical, sulking-then-blowing behavior pattern was in play, only now at a much more dramatic level. Any suggestion by his teacher that Tad participate, pay attention, or stop a behavior that was disruptive to the class would lead to a major explosion. Tad had been moved to the special day class, where he had only three classmates, lowered stimulation, and a teacher's aide. Within two weeks, his pregnant teacher actually quit her job, fearing she would be physically attacked by Tad. He had launched a chair on the day before she announced she would be leaving, narrowly missing her head.

Along with the school's principal, we were repeatedly called on to try and manage Tad's explosiveness, most times culminating in a "takedown," meaning Tad would have to be taken to the floor on his stomach and contained until he would eventually stop fighting. He'd become so exhausted by the outpouring of energy that he would inevitably fall asleep.

Tad's mother had begun individual counseling with Frank. This was a condition of family reunification, as was the requirement that Tad and his mother participate in weekly family counseling. In addition, Tad's mom was required to attend a parenting class.

As with Gabriel, we put a behavior plan together for Tad, including rewarding short periods of appropriate behavior. Once again the computer was used as a reward. On several occasions, Frank would take Tad off the school grounds to a local park, where they would talk about Tad's brief but encouraging successes. At the same time, Frank would do what he could to encourage Tad to talk about his feelings, particularly those brought about by his losses. But for Tad, relating his sadness and anger to the deaths of his "dads" or the mistreatment by his "caregivers," was just way too scary, and he resisted at every turn.

Like most eight-year-olds, Tad liked to draw. Frank asked Tad to draw a picture of his "relaxing place" using colorful markers and a regular-size piece of printer paper. Tad drew himself and his deceased step dad having a picnic in a lush green meadow, alongside a deep-blue river. There were singing birds in the air and a warm yellow sun overhead. Also suspended in the sky was a portrait of Tad's biological dad in stick figure, a pleasant smile taking up most of his face. And alongside him, the dog Tad had once loved and cared for. The picture was clear evidence of a boy trying to make peace with his losses, an attempt to blend what he had with what he'd lost.

When asked how he felt when he looked at his drawing, Tad would consistently answer, "good." When reminded that "good" isn't a feeling, Tad would remember the five feelings he'd explored with Frank earlier in his treatment, and then say, "happy" (See activity: I Know That Face).

Tad was encouraged to take a few deep breaths and try and relax his muscles. Then Frank would suggest that he and Tad sprawl out on the grass, side by side and faces toward the sky. Then Frank would hold the picture overhead where both could see it. Frank would put soothing words to the peaceful scene, noting the warm sun and the pleasant smell of the lush green grass. The pair would imagine the peaceful sound of the calmly flowing river as it moved confidently along its path. Tad would be encouraged to place his hand on his stomach and to breathe from deep down, so that he was aware of his belly protruding with each relaxing breath.

It was during these relaxation sessions that Tad was at his calmest. Frank taught Tad to "notice" his sense of calm, and how nice it felt, and he was taught to be able to re-create this feeling whenever he liked. Tad was encouraged to take his picture home and put it in a place where he would see it often. Tad decided on taping the drawing to the corner of his bedroom mirror, and he would take it down from time to time, when feeling a need to calm himself.

Tad's behavior at home improved markedly over the first few months that he participated in counseling. School, however, was a different story. Tad was labeled as Severely Emotionally Disturbed, and he was moved to a newly developed behavior class with just two other students. His behavior didn't improve, however, and he continued to lash out at other students and throw things at his new teacher. Even after being moved to this classroom where there was less stimulation, far fewer students, and a teacher's aide, Tad's behavior only worsened. He drew horrifying, black pictures of himself on fire and of his family members with their faces scribbled upon with black marker. Tad had become incapable of learning. His out-of-control emotions had taken over. The violent episodes continued, and the ferocity only worsened. Finally, the school's principal was forced to call a meeting, fearing that Tad's behavior would result in harm to himself, his classmates, or his teacher. We met with Tad's mother. Together it was decided that a group home and nonpublic school would be found, one that would give Tad much needed structure and immediate feedback for his behavior and that might help him manage his anger and control his impulses. A group home on a working cattle ranch was located in northern Colorado. It was run by a firm but compassionate husband and wife. There Tad would live in an old-style ranch house with nine other children, all experiencing behavior problems that kept them from their homes and families.

Still considered a resident of the county he came from, Frank was able to continue managing Tad's case, while Lynn Ann managed his education plan, as he took part in the group home's behavior program and nonpublic school. Unfortunately, even after several months, Tad continued to struggle with his behavior. He was provoking the other kids, refusing to take part in the program, and rarely if ever did he work his way up the "steps" of the program's level system before some ferocious episode would result in his tumbling back down the steps and having to start from the bottom once again.

Sadly, Tad's ongoing violent behavior resulted in his expulsion, first from one group home, then two more over the following few years. It seemed Tad was having an especially hard time managing his anger and his impulses, a trait not uncommon in kids with ADHD, particular when combined with posttraumatic stress. Still, it wasn't the norm to see little or no improvement in a child's behavior after several years of structured treatment and medication. No matter what the structure of the particular program, Tad was only becoming more violent and more resistant to working out his issues.

When Tad was 11 years old, the county was able to sponsor Tad in having a SPECT scan of his brain from Dr. Amen's clinic in Fairfield, California. The scan revealed an abnormality in the left temporal lobe of Tad's brain. More specifically, a "hot spot," meaning marked overactivity. The part of Tad's brain that was involved with aggression was over-*reacting*. The Amen Clinic recommended a mood stabilizing medication, and Tad was immediately started on Depakote.

Sadly, within a matter of days and before the medication had a chance to rise to a therapeutic level in Tad's blood, he viciously assaulted a staff member while riding in the van to school. Frank received a phone call from the group home manager first, then a call from the district attorney of the county where Tad had been living. It seemed his violent behavior had escalated to the point of attracting the attention of the juvenile justice system. County mental health and the local school district would no longer be calling the shots.

Frank made sure that the court was made aware of the abnormal brain scan and about the medication recommended by the Amen Clinic. A copy of the clinic report was faxed to Tad's probation officer, but our hands were tied. We could only watch from a distance . . . and hope.

What We Learned from Tad

We learned firsthand from Tad how childhood trauma can affect a child so deeply that the emotional scarring may be irreversible. We wondered whether the abnormality found in Tad's brain was a result of psychological trauma or, if he was born with a defective brain, how responsible was that defect for his behavior problems?

At about the same time, we became aware of the work of Bruce Perry (discussed in Chapter 2) and his research on the impact of trauma on the brains of children. From Tad, we learned firsthand the irreversible effects of violence on the life of a child.

Our time with Tad served as a reminder of the importance of family members' and caregivers' timely cooperation in the treatment and education of their children. Tad's young life had been a living hell, and only much later were the quantity and severity of the life-altering traumas more fully revealed. Despite the chaos, Tad had somehow become a compassionate and sensitive boy, able to melt your heart in one moment and make your blood run cold the next. As passionate as we had become about wanting to help him heal and learn, we were forced to accept our powerlessness and watch him enter "the system," where the realistic goal seems to be not so much healing the child as protecting society from the child's inability to manage his aggressive behavior.

We learned from Tad the importance of current and future brain research, and we've begun to put our hope and faith in the future science and technology that will someday result in early diagnosis and more effective treatment for children like him.

Tad will always have a place in our hearts, and he'll forever be a part of our work.

Tad's is a story of grief and inspiration.

Jeremy

Frank received a call from a foster mom who lived in a home deep among the pines very near his office. He'd known Dorie for years. She was a caring Native Americn woman with grown kids of her own. Her husband was a traditional native man, tall and soft-spoken, and he lived for hunting deer and rabbits.

Dorie and John had taken in a 12-year-old boy, placed with them by a neighboring county's family service agency. Dorie described Jeremy as pleasant enough, but he'd had an episode the night before that caused her concern. It seemed she'd found feces smeared along the bathroom sink and toilet bowl. Dorie was experienced enough with children to know that sometimes the smearing of feces was a glaring indication of a child in emotional trouble.

Dorie informed Frank that she and John had taken Jeremy in two weeks prior. Frank got what history he could from Dorie and asked about the other foster kids in the home. Before hanging up, he scheduled to meet with Jeremy the following day, and he jotted down the name and number of Jeremy's social worker in the neighboring county. Frank was happy to hear that his case worker was a woman he'd worked with before and for whom he had a great deal of respect.

Frank phoned Donna and took a history on Jeremy over the phone. Both Jeremy and an older brother, Donnie, were removed from the home after his mother was arrested for the second time for possession of methamphetamine and failure to comply with a family reunification plan, which included completing a drug treatment program. Donnie had a long history of petty crimes, so Donna had decided to place him and Jeremy in separate foster homes in different counties. Jeremy's dad was in county jail for a drug conviction and for domestic violence on Jeremy's mom. Jeremy's oldest brother, Michael, had been killed on the streets a year prior in an apparently random act of senseless violence. Jeremy had been the first person to reach Michael as he lay dying in the street.

Jeremy walked to my office on the following day. In the lobby, Frank greeted a somewhat chubby, crew-cutted boy with a sly smile and a glint in his eye.

In our first session Frank explained to Jeremy that his job was to help kids and families solve problems by getting to know the kids that he saw. Frank asked Jeremy if he would let him get to know him, and Jeremy said, "sure."

Jeremy openly talked with Frank about his family and the death of his brother without a hint of emotion. He let him know that his father was violent and deserved to be in jail. He spoke of his mother as a victim of circumstances, and he defended her at every opportunity. He had no complaints about living in Dorie and John's home, and he hoped he'd be able to go back to his mom soon. He added, "she needs me."

Frank asked Jeremy about what Dorie had found on the bathroom sink and rim of the toilet bowl. Jeremy looked a little embarrassed and told him that it had been an accident.

"I fell asleep in the bathtub," he said, "and when I woke up, I'd had an accident. I tried to move it to the toilet but I guess I didn't do a very good job."

Even though Jeremy seemed to have a right to the kind of rage that is often underlying a behavior like smearing feces, he seemed sincere in his explanation. The more glaring concerns were his complete denial of any emotion concerning the dysfunction in his family and the abandonment Frank suspected he felt but couldn't express.

In a phone conversation with his fifth-grade teacher, Frank learned that Jeremy had a very hard time concentrating on his work, rarely completing an assignment. He'd been tested for a learning disability, but no obvious learning handicap was found, and he didn't qualify for special education. His teacher and Frank suspected his attention problem might be stress related, and they decided to compare notes again in a few weeks after Jeremy had a chance to settle in at school and had a few more counseling sessions under his belt. The possibility of ADHD was in the back of both their minds.

Over the next few weeks, Frank learned that Jeremy and his mother had done a classic role reversal. He was her main source of emotional support, and Jeremy had to stay "strong" for his mom. Frank asked for more specific information about the death of his brother, Michael. Jeremy explained that he and Michael had been playing videogames together. When they had finished, Michael had headed down the street toward a buddy's house. A few minutes later, a neighbor raced to Jeremy's front door and shouted at him that someone had shot Michael on the street. Jeremy got to Michael first and held him as he died. He told Frank that when his mother arrived on the scene she was hysterical. Jeremy held and comforted his mother without shedding a tear.

Frank began to subtly suggest to Jeremy that many of the events that had occurred in his life were likely to give rise to some emotion. Initially, any such suggestions from Frank were met with silence and that endearing sly smile. Any intervention as direct as "what was that like for you?" or "how did you feel about that?" was met with a purely cognitive response, in simpler terms, a *thought* rather than a *feeling*. "How did it feel to see your dad hitting your mom?" "I wanted him to leave," or "we didn't need him around." It had quickly become obvious that denial had been an unspoken rule in Jeremy's home, not uncommon in families where physical and substance abuse is occurring. A result is often an unwillingness to recognize and express emotions.

Without realizing it, Jeremy had found it necessary to carve out his role as mom's caretaker amid the chaos. And to be effective in that role, it would be necessary to set all of his emotions aside. Frank's concern for Jeremy was that he'd gotten to be so good at concealing what he was feeling that he no longer *knew* what he was feeling. And if he didn't know, he had no way of expressing it. Without healthy ways to express his feelings, he was at risk of going into emotional overload. He would be a prime candidate to take the popular "quick-and-easy" path to relieving stress: drug abuse or some other form of addiction. Or possibly he would eventually create a "family" for himself by joining a gang.

Jeremy's initial work in counseling was to learn the difference between a thought and a feeling (see activity: Think It or Feel It). Weeks of conversation followed, and progress was made. Jeremy got into the habit of glancing at a felt wall hanging Frank kept in his office containing five round clown faces for help. Each face expressed a different emotion: happy, sad, angry, scared, and confused. When Frank would ask a "feelings" question, Jeremy would glance at the wall, then give me that smile of his, and answer using words he'd find on the wall.

"How are you feeling about your mom going back to jail?" "Sad and confused." Jeremy decided it was particularly cool that he could have more than one feeling at a time. Not having this knowledge prior had been another confusing feelings-related issue that contributed to his decision to just not deal with the darn things at all.

Jeremy was encouraged to talk about his feelings in a safe and nurturing environment (see activity: When Feelings Take Shape). After a few months, it became clear that his mother was completely unwilling to follow the court's family reunification plan, and Jeremy knew that as long as she refused, he would not be returned to her.

His usual cool and protective attitude toward his mother began to gradually change. He was soon in touch with his sadness and anger over her unwillingness to fight for reunification.

He was able to finally begin grieving the death of his brother, initially drawing pictures of the two of them competing ferociously at videogames, then eventually, of Michael in Heaven, riding his Harley, something Jeremy figured Michael would spend his time doing if Heaven was all it was cracked up to be.

Jeremy's concentration problems at school were soon under control, as the anxiety he was using to keep a lid on his feelings was resolved and his energy could be used for more productive tasks, like focusing on his assignments until they were completed.

Eighteen months after first meeting Jeremy, he went to live with his father who had served out his sentence, completed a drug program and anger management, found a job, and rented a house, specifically so that he and Jeremy could be reunited.

Jeremy was able to tell Frank and his social worker, in no certain terms, that going to live with his dad in the city made him feel a little bit scared and a whole lot happy.

What We Learned from Jeremy

Jeremy was a timely reminder that not every child with attention problems suffers from ADHD nor should every one be medicated. At the risk of repeating ourselves, every child needs to be viewed as an individual, within the context of his or her life experience. A parent, teacher, or counselor's best ally in understanding the child's needs is the child himself.

Jeremy's opportunity to be a child had been taken from him by the adults whose job it was to nurture and protect him. Under debilitating stress and lacking the necessary coping skills, Jeremy had gone into survival mode. On some level, he determined that his survival and the survival of his mother was dependent on his strength and his denial of the true extent of the chaos at hand.

We were reminded of the importance of a child staying in touch with his or her feelings and of having at least one adult around who is willing to hear about them.

In his foster home, Jeremy was allowed to be a child again. It would be up to his mother and father to succeed or fail on their own, without their 12-year-old son to act as protector or scapegoat.

About two-thirds of the way through the counseling process, Jeremy told Frank about a dream he'd had a few nights before. In the dream, he drove a tram through the underground sewer system while wearing a clown suit. His job, he said, was to clean the sewer with a long, heavy mop along his route. We explored his thoughts and feeling about the dream in detail. When we'd finished, Jeremy concluded that the dream represented the job he'd taken on in his family, before he'd gone into foster care. His job had been to clean up the messes while wearing a smile.

We'll always remember that sly smile.

5

About Learning Styles

O ver the years, you may have noticed that it's easier for you to learn in some ways and more difficult in others. For example, you may have had difficulty learning to cook by looking at cookbook recipes, then realized the process was easier and more enjoyable if your mother walked you through it on the phone. If so, it's likely that you are a strong *verbal-linguistic* learner (learn by listening) or a strong *interpersonal* learner (learn by interacting with others), and not as strong in the *visual-spatial* style of learning (learning by watching, looking at diagrams, etc). Or maybe the combination of interacting with your mother (interpersonal) and listening (verbal-linguistic) to her explain as she went along was the ideal combination of teaching methods for you as *an individual*. We will focus on the seven different learning strengths in this chapter (Gardner, 2006;[1] Armstrong,[2] 1993).

---

[1] Howard Gardner identified an eighth intelligence, Naturalist Intelligence, in his book *Multiple Intelligences: New Horizons* in 2006, and we will discuss this intelligence later in this chapter. This most recently identified intelligence, while certainly worth discussion and further research, lacks specific relevance for our purposes, and we've chosen not to use it in the activities contained here.

[2] The authors greatly respect the work of Thomas Armstrong in the area of multiple intelligence, and we highly recommend his book *Seven Kinds of Smart* (1993), which we've drawn upon in developing the exercises contained here. We wish to make clear that Dr. Armstrong believes strongly that ADD and ADHD are myths and "serve as a neat way to explain the complexities of turn-of-the millennium life in America" (Myth of ADD: www.ThomasArmstrong.com). We respect Dr. Armstrong's views, and as we told him in an e-mail discussion during the writing of this book, our intent is to share our positive experiences in teaching challenging children social skills and improve their ability to manage their emotions regardless of what label has been put

On the other hand, maybe you have had difficulty learning to work on cars by listening to your father explain as he worked, finding it easier to understand the tasks after finding a shop manual with loads of diagrams and schematics of how things worked and how to fix them. If so, it's likely that you are a *visual-spatial* learner. Or, maybe *bodily-kinesthetic* (physical/hands-on) activities are difficult for you, and the physical aspects of auto mechanics don't come easily. But by calling upon your individual learning style (visual-spatial), you were able to learn and retain more than you would have otherwise. Has your child been given the advantage of being taught about expressing feelings and managing behavior with consideration for his or her *individual* learning style? Probably not . . . until now.

Each of us has certain strengths that we use in our daily lives to learn and accomplish daily tasks. We may be very strong in one or two styles and not as strong in others. The following will help you to understand the seven learning styles used in this book to help your child learn about feelings, improve his or her behavior, and lessen the symptoms of ADHD.

Overview of the Seven Strengths

Logical-Mathematical (The Problem Solver)

Logical-Mathematical intelligence is the ability to manipulate numbers and use logic to solve problems. This learning style first appears when a child begins to show interest in counting his or her fingers and toes, building with blocks, stacking toys, or in other ways exploring the world of objects and numbers and manipulating them toward a desired effect. Howard Gardner (1983) writes, "For it is in confronting objects, in ordering and reordering them, and in assessing their quantity, that the young child gains his or her initial and most fundamental knowledge about the logical-mathematical realm." Logical-mathematical intelli-

upon them. The ADHD controversy, we believe, is best addressed by the scientists. The authors hope that this book serves as inspiration for you the reader to research the matter further and to form your own opinion.

gence is responsible for the various patterns of thinking we use in our daily lives, such as setting priorities or making lists. Traits of a logical-mathematically inclined person include the abilities to reason, to predict what will result from a particular action, and to use numbers to understand, organize, and learn about things. This is the intelligence of the computer programmer, the scientist, and accountant. The child who is a strong logical-mathematical learner is likely to enjoy solving problems, organizing items, performing experiments, or working with numbers.

Bodily-Kinesthetic (The Physical Learner)

This is the intelligence of the physical self. Gardner writes "characteristics of such intelligence is the ability to use one's body in highly differentiated and skilled ways, for expressive as well as goal-directed purposes." Mechanics, surgeons, carpenters, and athletes are likely to possess this type of intelligence, "so too did Charlie Chaplin, who drew upon it in order to perform his many ingenious routines as the "little tramp" (Armstrong, 1993). The younger reader might be more familiar with the physical talents of star basketball player Michael Jordan or golfer Annika Sorenstam. Kids strong in the bodily-kinesthetic learning style are likely to display talent in handling objects and controlling body movements, and they are likely to enjoy physical activities, such as dancing, acting, or playing physical pretend games, including play-fighting or tag. This child is likely to be very physically active and generally prefers to be outdoors. The authors have found a large percentage of kids diagnosed with ADHD (the predominantly hyperactive and impulsive type) to have been happiest when being physical, and they are likely to be strong bodily-kinesthetic learners.

Intrapersonal (Knows Thyself)

This is the intelligence of the inner self. The central feature of this intelligence is the capacity to tell the difference among feelings, to name them, and to use them as a way of understanding and managing one's behavior. David Lazear (1994) writes, "As far as we know, we are the only creatures gifted with such an ability. Intrapersonal intelligence involves knowledge about an awareness of the internal aspects of the self such as feeling, thinking processes, self-reflection, and intuition about spiritual realities." Counselors, ministers, and self-employed businesspeople are likely to have strong intrapersonal intelligence. The child who is a strong intrapersonal learner is likely to enjoy spending time alone, learning about feelings, or hearing or writing about the inner workings of others.

Interpersonal (Relates Well to Others)

This is the ability to relate to other people. An interpersonally intelligent individual can view the world from another's point of view. This intelligence uses our ability to communicate both with and without words and allows for the ability to distinguish among moods, temperament, intentions, and motivations. "An interpersonally intelligent individual may be very compassionate and socially responsible like Mahatma Gandhi, or manipulative and cunning like Machiavelli" (Armstrong, 1993). A teacher, politician, therapist, or negotiator is likely to be interpersonally intelligent. A child who is a strong interpersonal learner is likely to show interest in the actions and ideas of others, enjoy listening to or reading about others, and be interested in learning how he or she may be like or different from others.

Musical-Rhythmic (Likes Rhythms and Rhymes)

Musical intelligence is the ability to perceive, enjoy, and produce rhythms, melodies, and rhymes. According to Gardner, of all the gifts with which individuals may be endowed, none emerges earlier than musical talent. He goes on to write, "the various lines of evidence that I have reviewed . . . suggest that, like language, music is a separate intellectual competence, one that is also not dependent upon physical objects in the world" (1983). According to Lazear (1994), this intelligence is active when we use tones and rhythmic patterns to communicate how we are feeling and what we believe or to express the depth of our religious devotion or the intensity of our national loyalty. The child who is a strong musical-rhythmic learner is likely to appreciate music, rhymes, and jingles. He or she most likely has a favorite song and has most likely memorized its words.

Visual-Spatial (Seeing Is Believing)

This is the ability to think in pictures and to perceive and re-create the visual-spatial world. People with high visual-spatial intelligence are often very sensitive to visual detail and can easily memorize what they see. They are likely to enjoy drawing or painting, and they can orient themselves in three-dimensional space with ease. We show this intelligence when we use a map or read a blueprint. It follows, then, that individuals with visual-spatial intelligence are likely to become architects, photographers, artists, pilots, or mechanical engineers. Kids with this type of intelligence often enjoy activities such as daydreaming, pretending to be invisible, imagining themselves to be on a great adventure to a magical place, or drawing or coloring.

Verbal-Linguistic (Has a Way with Words)

This is the intelligence of words. Perhaps the most universal of the seven learning strengths, verbal-linguistic intelligence has traditionally been one of the most highly valued in our modern society. This is probably why the IQ test draws heavily upon verbal ability. We use this intelligence when we speak to each other and when we put our thoughts down on paper, write poetry, and use metaphors, analogies, or puns. Armstrong writes, "but the most important component of linguistic intelligence is the capacity to use language to achieve practical goals. The language may not be dazzling or first-rate, but the purpose to which language is bent serves to enhance, or at the very least, to change lives in some tangible way" (1993). Writers, lawyers, and journalists are likely to possess high verbal-linguistic intelligence. Children who possess this learning strength are likely to enjoy listening to and telling stories, keeping journals, debating about their beliefs, and having fun with word games.

Naturalist (Connected to Nature)

People who possess this learning strength have a connection with the natural world. They enjoy animals, the outdoors, and have evolved sensory perceptual ability. They tend to take a keen interest in such subjects as biology, botany, geology, zoology, astronomy, meteorology, and paleontology. These people will notice patterns, subtle changes in weather, and are good at categorizing and cataloging items. They may enjoy collecting and have a fascination at an early age, with fossils, shells, bugs, feathers, butterflies, and rocks. These kids have "nature smarts"

Why You Should Know about Learning Strengths

Does it really matter in what way knowledge is conveyed? Is paying attention to a child's individual learning strengths really important? The fact is that a child will learn and retain more information if he or she is regarded as an individual rather than as a member of the teacher's student body, or the counselor's caseload (Gardner, 1983; Armstrong, 1993; Lazear, 1994). By late in the twentieth century, most teachers, particularly those who taught kids with learning disabilities, had realized that teaching by lecture (talking at students) just wasn't achieving the desired results. Kids weren't learning up to their potential, and teachers and students alike had become frustrated by what amounted to an academic "disconnect." Teachers, often strong *verbal-linguistic* learners, were most likely teaching students using the same methods that were used in teaching *them*. And they were teaching material in the way that *they* were most comfortable, without much, if any, consideration for the ways their individual students *learned* best.

Fortunately, partially because of the work of researchers and scholars such as Howard Gardner and Thomas Armstrong in the 1980s and 1990s, teachers began to take note of individual learning styles and apply them in their classrooms. Our experience has taught us that identifying and using a child's individual learning styles makes the teaching and counseling of kids far more successful. Interestingly, entire schools, such as the Key Learning Community in Indianapolis, that focus on individual learning differences have sprung up from scratch, and hundreds of schools around the world claim to be implementing multiple intelligence theory (Gardner, 2006). The term "learning style" is meant to describe not only the particular way that the child learns best, but just as importantly, the style of learning that is particularly interesting to the child.

Think about it. If a child has a natural interest in dinosaurs, for example, is he likely to be willing to listen to you talk about a day in the life of a T-Rex? Why? Because the subject interests him. Likewise, if you need to teach your child about staying calm in a stressful situation, you'd better have a way of broaching the subject in a way that will hold his interest (such as using a *visual-spatial*, or *bodily-kinesthetic* style). Talking at him about the subject will most likely make for a very short and unproductive session. Once you've figured out how to keep your child interested, imagine being able to present the "lesson" in the way he learns best. That's precisely what we've done in this book, and we've applied these same methods with the kids we've taught and counseled, and with remarkable success.

Now, you as the helper have a double advantage in getting the material across to your child. By identifying and using your child's individual learning styles, you will be able to hold his or her interest and teach him or her in the way he or she learns best. Special educators in particular, that tireless and resilient breed that we look to for meeting the special educational needs of our kids with learning disabilities, have outpaced the rest of us in using individual learning strengths and interests to their students' advantage. Because kids qualifying for special education services, especially ADHD kids, rarely learn best by language, that is "listening or reading," the payoff from utilizing individual learning styles has rendered particularly significant rewards in these special education classrooms.

A study to determine whether teachers trained in individual learning style considerations will result in improved student outcomes, as compared to teachers who are not, was conducted at Sanford Middle School in the Lee County, Alabama, school system over the 1994/1995 and 1995/1996 school years. Reading, language, and science regular classroom teachers attended a two-day workshop on learning styles, while math and social studies teachers did not. The Stanford Achievement Test was administered to 120 fifth graders prior to their teachers attending the workshop, and then to the same students the next year while in the 6th grade. A summary of the results follows in Table 5-1.

Table 5-1. Impact of teachers trained in learning styles: An informal study.

	5th grade	6th grade
*Reading	40th percentile,	70th percentile
Math	44th percentile,	40th percentile
*Language	50th percentile,	71st percentile
*Science	47th percentile,	78th percentile
Social Studies	43rd percentile,	39th percentile

From Williams 2007.

Yet, we now find ourselves close to the end of the first decade of the twenty-first century, and where is that *activity* book for kids with learning problems that teaches them about feelings and how to manage their behavior using their individual learning strengths and interests? Well, finally, you have it in your hands.

Some famous and amazingly successful people throughout history had difficulty learning the way that others insisted on teaching them. Winston Churchill had problems in reading and suffered from a speech impediment. He was so behind that he was placed in the section of his class where the "slow" boys were taught English. Albert Einstein was considered a daydreamer by his teachers, and he actually failed several math classes as a boy. Louis Pasteur failed the entrance exams to medical school, and his father considered him stupid. And Woodrow Wilson, who eventually went on to become the twenty-seventh president of the United States, was not able to learn the letters of the alphabet until he was nine years old.

On a recent episode of CBS's *Late Late Show with Craig Ferguson,* filmmaker Quentin Tarantino confided that he never spent one day in high school, having quit middle school at age 15. He considered teaching to have been performed like a cattle operation, in which you either went with the herd or you were left behind. He was one in the herd who couldn't keep up. Because he couldn't keep up, he decided that he was the "dumb kid." He didn't like that very much, so he refused to attend.

How creative and competent do you suppose a filmmaker needs to be to be responsible for such movies as *Pulp Fiction, Reservoir Dogs,* and *Jackie Brown,* to name just three of Tarantino's films, earning many millions in box office revenue? Do you suppose young Tarantino was a strong visual-spatial learner even in middle school? And how about possessing the natural problem-solving business skills (logical-mathematical learning style) it takes to create and direct successful high-budget major motion pictures? How about interpersonal skills? Do you imagine a film director, whose job it is to direct the acting of major movie stars (and their egos), has some strength in that area (interpersonal learning style)?

It's fairly obvious in listening to Mr. Tarantino that he's probably not naturally strong in the verbal-linguistic style of learning, or at least not in the traditional sense (this is also generally true of ADHD-labeled kids), and we're betting that was his undoing in middle school. Interestingly, Tarantino, whose films are frequently described as offbeat and "nonlinear," wrote his first screenplay at age 14, just before leaving school for good, and went on to win an Academy Award in the best original screenplay category for *Pulp Fiction* in 1994. It would follow, then, that Tarantino did (and does) possess verbal-linguistic skills. Perhaps it was his uniqueness, his individuality, that led to being left behind in school. Was anyone paying attention to that individuality? To how he *could* learn?

Quentin Tarantino found a way to be successful despite the system's unwillingness to view him as an individual child and not just one of the herd, and we commend him for his tenacity (perhaps there should be a ninth learning style, The Tenacious Learner). Unfortunately, he could be the poster boy for representing the exception to the rule. We encourage school systems to rethink their unwillingness to see students as individuals with various strengths, including learning strengths, to value all of them, and to show some creativity in teaching them accordingly.

No matter what their specific learning difficulties, all of the individuals mentioned above learned to compensate by drawing on their individual talents and learning styles. Cheri Fuller writes in *Unlocking Your Child's Learning Potential,* "What mattered most for each of them was focusing and capitalizing on their strengths, developing a vision and hope for the future, and applying the determination and perseverance to do what it took to reach their goals" (1994).

We're fairly certain these remarkable people also had at least one person in their lives who valued them as individuals and encouraged them to use their individual learning strengths to accomplish their dreams. We wish the same for your child.

CHAPTER 6

Survival Skills 101 for Parents, Teachers, and Counselors

Parents of ADHD kids are three times more likely to divorce than other married people in the general population (Amen, 2001).

Evelyn and Kevin Hollister are the parents of Steven, 10, and Michelle, 12. Kevin works as a marketing executive for a computer software company, and Evelyn works part-time as a medical social worker. Kevin and Evelyn are well educated, and the family's socioeconomic status is upper middle class. Outwardly, the Hollister's appear to be the ideal American family.

Why, then, over the past few years, has Evelyn had to change jobs several times, prompted by less-than-flattering performance evaluations? Most of these focused on her frequent tardiness and inconsistent attendance.

Kevin has been bypassed for promotions because of his unwillingness to travel with the frequency expected of him by the vice president of his company. Over the past two years, he's seen his family doctor twice as often as in the past, usually complaining of stomach problems and fatigue.

Michelle, considered the "perfect child" until recently by her parents, has seemingly become overly sensitive and has begun to "talk back." Michelle's teacher has begun sending notes home from school, indicating Michelle seems sullen and has been withdrawing from her friends.

A closer look reveals a family pushed to the limit by Steven's attention and behavior problems. Evelyn now starts her day an hour earlier than necessary in an effort to allow Steven extra time to get ready for school. In the process, she denies herself an hour of sleep on a regu-

69

lar basis. But, no matter how much time is allowed, Steven still isn't able to organize himself in the morning. He takes 20 minutes to wash up, brush his teeth, and comb his hair, and another 20 minutes to dress. Evelyn checks on Steven's progress several times, but most of the time she finds him in the middle of a totally unrelated activity, such as flipping through baseball cards, jumping on his bed, or preparing to fire up a videogame. After a verbal battle and momentary redirection by his mom, Steven will be lucky to remain on task for more than a couple of minutes at a time.

During breakfast, Evelyn and Kevin repeatedly nag Steven to help keep him focused. But Steven still can't quite make the bus most mornings, and Evelyn has to drive 15 minutes out of her way to get Steven to school.

Once Steven comes home from school and has a snack, Evelyn sits with him at the kitchen table to help him organize his homework. What should take 45 minutes takes Steven nearly two hours most evenings, and the Evelyn finds the effort required to repeatedly drag Steven's attention back to his work exhausting.

Any attempt by Michelle to get needed attention from her mom is met with impatience. "Can't you see I'm trying to get your brother to do his homework?" And a chastised Michelle withdraws further into her own world.

By the time Kevin gets home from work, the tension in the house can be cut with a knife, and all Evelyn can think about is getting through the dinner dishes and going to bed.

Midway through the fourth grade, Steven has already been suspended three times. Two were for angry outbursts that escalated to outright aggression; the third was after he refused to participate in class and then offered up a few choice words for the principal. In a meeting with Steven's parents, his teacher described him as "irritable, uncooperative, and bouncing off the walls."

At this point, Evelyn and Kevin elected to seek medical attention and counseling for their son, and they began looking for ways for Steven to exercise his frontal lobes and lessen his symptoms of ADHD. But, they also need to consider taking care of themselves. In meeting the challenge of providing for their son, how would they cope?

The Dos and Don'ts of Coping

Rest. Proper rest and sufficient sleep are essential fo
body and mind. Meeting the challenges of reachin
ADHD child is time consuming, but cutting corner
egy that's likely to backfire. Sleep deprivation is often accompanied by
irritability, confusion, fatigue, and depression. This results in a mental
state incompatible with the task at hand. Insufficient rest and sleep can
also weaken the immune system and leave people more vulnerable to
sickness and disease.

Watch the caffeine. Relying on caffeine and sugar to get going in the
morning results in a big dip in energy level well before lunch. With the
blahs comes the temptation to "coffee-up" once again, only perpetuating
the cycle. And what's more, relying on coffee for energy as the day pro-
gresses will jeopardize the ability to get a good night's sleep (see above!)

Get physical. Exercise rids the body of stress hormones and pro-
duces natural pain killers called endorphins (literal translation: internal
morphine). The increase in blood flow that comes with exercise also
makes your brain work better. To be efficient, your brain needs good
blood flow for carrying in nutrition and carrying away waste. An added
bonus is the boost in self-esteem and confidence that comes with looking good and being in shape.

Watch the alcohol. The idea of having a few drinks to relax in a hurry
can be tempting. But before you do, consider that alcohol is a central
nervous system depressant and can add to the depressed mood that you
might be experiencing as a result of the stress. Also, too much alcohol
(as with caffeine) will restrict blood flow to the brain, hindering your
ability to think clearly—and not only while under the influence.

Drink plenty of water. Your brain is about 80 percent water. If you
don't replenish your body's water supply, your brain won't work at its best.

Get enough good fats. The majority of your brain's dry weight is
made up of fat, and your brain relies on fat to operate properly. Good
fats, such as omega-3 fatty acids, are found in fish or in supplements,
both in pill and liquid form. Without proper intake of healthy fats, your
brain will rely on saturated fats, like the gross goo that bubbles to the
surface of a frying hamburger patty. If required to rely on this kind of

...dge, you can expect your brain to be sluggish. If your brain is sluggish, you will be too.

Go for the high-octane fuel. Green leafy vegetables and other colorful foods like berries and beets contain vitamins and minerals that are good for the brain. It may be tempting to rely on comfort foods that are high in sugar content and empty calories when feeling stressed, but every effort should be made to eat these foods only sparingly, if at all.

Connect socially. It's important to make frequent contact with people you enjoy being around, and its okay to avoid people who bring you down. Over the years we've surveyed hundreds of people and asked what makes them happy. The number one answer by far has consistently been, "being with people I like."

Keep learning. You're doing that right at this moment. Your brain was designed for learning, and learning makes for a happy brain. A happy brain makes for a happy person. Music is a particularly good method of exercising the brain, be it learning an instrument or practicing dance steps. Music is thought to exercise more than one brain system at a time.

Nurture your spirit. Whatever does this for you personally, from church to fishing, find a way to help center yourself in your world.

Make a deal with your spouse. Schedule a break for yourself at a time when your partner can take over for you. If an overnight getaway isn't in the cards, take a few hours and go do something you enjoy. A short break doesn't have to involve spending a lot of money. You might decide to take a scenic drive, do some window shopping, or get together with a buddy and hit some golf balls. It's a good idea to schedule these breaks ahead of time, so that when things are heating up at home, you can look forward to your "me time."

Lighten up. Forgive yourself for giving extra attention to your child with behavior problems. It has nothing to do with favoring one child over the rest, and there's no reason to feel guilty. At the same time, be sure the other kids understand that they are every bit as important. Make every effort to spend one-on-one time with the kids that might be feeling less special. You will be surprised how far 15 minutes of individual time twice a week can go. Activities you can do together include reading a book, doing a puzzle, or just listening. This time together can go a long way in making the other kids sure they are loved just as much. Make the other kids a part of the helping process for the ADHD-labeled child. Talk to them individually about their learning strengths and explain what a big help it would be to you if they would take a little time to use those strengths in helping their brother or sister. "Michelle, you're so good with your times tables. I'll bet you'd make a great teacher for Steven. Do you think you could make up some flashcards?"

Lastly, avoid power struggles with your kids. Easier said than done, we realize, but arguing with your challenging child or getting worked up when things are going wrong will lead to the exact opposite result from the one you're looking for. We'll be discussing this in more detail in Chapter 7.

Whether the parent, teacher, or counselor of a challenging child, if you're healthy in mind, body, and spirit you will be better able to help your kids, and the above strategies apply.

A Special Note to Counselors and Special Educators: Burnout and Secondary Posttraumatic Stress Disorder (PTSD)

By now you're most likely familiar with the much-publicized term "secondary PTSD," sometimes referred to as burnout. These terms describe a condition in which individuals experience emotional trauma secondhand. Unfortunately, it's a fairly common occurrence among helping professionals. Some of the symptoms of secondary PTSD include emotional exhaustion, fatigue, decreased job satisfaction, depressed mood, and somatic complaints, such as stomach problems or frequent headaches (Kanel, 2006).

Research indicates that the best way to avoid or combat secondary PTSD is to open up a dialog with coworkers who have an accurate sense of what it is you do and what it's like to do it. Feeling isolated during the helping process seems to be a major contributing factor to bringing on the condition. If an informal, "over-coffee" conversation with a trusted coworker doesn't seem like enough of what you need, consider a more formalized get together, say for one hour on Tuesdays before quitting time. Employers are beginning to see the usefulness of allowing their employees time to provide support for each other. Doing so is likely to result in fewer sick days and stress leaves, and the end result will likely be a happier and healthier workforce providing better services to kids.

But don't stop there. Be sure to maintain healthy boundaries for yourself. No matter how important your work, it's still your work, not your entire life. Find satisfaction in small successes. Accept that sometimes that's all you're going to get. And without your hard work, even those wouldn't have been achieved.

Lastly, and maybe most importantly of all, create balance in your life. Think of yourself as a bank account. When you put energy into helping someone else, it's like making a withdrawal. When you do something to nurture yourself, it's like making a deposit. What kind of shape is your bank account in? Are you maintaining a healthy balance . . . or are you overdrawn?

CHAPTER 7

Reaching the Challenging Child— and Avoiding the Traps

K
ids labeled with ADHD and those with other types of frontal lobe problems are often blessed with an abundance of energy. Most likely, your first thought after reading the preceding sentence was something like "blessed?" or "Oh, he has an abundance of the stuff all right." Well, we *get* it, because we've *seen* it in the hundreds of kids we've taught and counseled. But we've also seen the majority of these kids learn to better focus that amazing energy and, when they did, we'd see amazing things happen. Once focused, the special qualities of these kids shone through, and they turned out to be some of the smartest, most curious, creative, talented, and athletic kids. Even with improved focus, however, they may have continued to struggle in school, particularly if the classroom was a tightly controlled *farmer* environment without consideration for the *hunter* brain (see Chapter 2).

Dr. Russell Barkley refers to kids labeled as ADHD as having a "disorder of self-control," and oftentimes overwhelmed by their own energy or intensity. Barkley recognized the impact of ADHD behavior on families, which include "sadness, frustration, guilt, stress, and marital strains" (1998). As a result, he introduced a Parent Training model. Barkley notes that of children diagnosed with ADHD and put on medication, 10 to 20 percent show no real improvement. Even when the medication does reduce symptoms, many children aren't able to handle the side effects. He notes a third group of children, whose parents decide not to seriously consider medication for their children, despite the probability that symptoms will be improved. Whether their children belong to one of these three groups or the group whose children actually benefit from medication, Barkley believes parents of all families that include an ADHD child can benefit from parent training. Barkley notes that parents of ADHD kids often become "overly-directive and negative in their parenting style," and often see themselves as less skilled and less knowledgeable in their parenting roles.

With this in mind, Barkley designed an 8- to 12-session parenting program that is conducted by a qualified therapist well versed on ADHD and intended to give parents the skills and knowledge to bring their hyperactive-impulsive child's behavior under control. The model is a ten-step process that ranges from educating parents on the reasons ADHD kids misbehave to instituting a daily school behavior report card for improving school behavior from home. Readers interested in more information on Barkley's parenting program should do some independent research and decide whether the program, or something similar, is for them. If so, consider finding a therapist trained in the model or one with experience working with parents of kids labeled ADHD.

Howard Glasser compares a child labeled with ADHD to a Mercedes Benz with the brakes of a Model T (1998). They have plenty of get up and go, but they lack the internal restraints to put the brakes on all that horsepower. So, in teaching these kids to have social skills, to anticipate consequences, to see themselves situationally, that is, to drag them over to their frontal lobes (the purpose of this book), what's the best approach?

First off, don't reward the problem behaviors. In *Transforming the Difficult Child* (1998), Glasser writes about some of the special considerations necessary when trying to reach and teach the "intense" child. The intense, highly energetic child craves stimulation. He pays little if any attention to the humdrum. But put him in charge of his own entertainment and he'll find what's loud, fast, and exciting. Right? Maybe you've noticed.

"Our children aren't out to get us. They are out to get our energy" (1998). Glasser compares us to our children's toys, noting that while they may have a number of features, *we* have thousands, including a wide range of moods and emotions, a variety of actions and reactions, and even a volume control. When our child causes a problem (pushes the right button), we turn on all the bells and whistles, thereby giving the child exactly what he craves. Glasser writes, "The energy, reactivity, and animation that we radiate when we are pleased is relatively flat compared to our verbal and nonverbal responses to behaviors that cause us displeasure, frustration, or anger." With this in mind, consider how easy it is for a child to conclude that this "toy" operates in much more entertaining ways when things are going wrong.

So notice the small successes and crank up the enthusiasm when pointing them out to your child. "You remembered to use your words when Sally took your pencil. That's fantastic! I'm really proud of you." Conversely (with little or no emotion and at a low volume), "uh-oh, you forgot to use your words, that's a ten-minute time out."

You are most likely familiar with the behavior management tool introduced by psychologist and lecturer Thomas Phelan called 1-2-3 Magic. The technique involves calmly counting to three if your child is unwilling to stop a behavior that you would like him to stop. For example, Tommy says, "Can I spend the night at Ryan's tonight? His parents said "It's okay." You might respond, "Not on a school night honey, maybe on Saturday." Tommy begins to plead. "Oh, please? I promise I'll get to sleep early . . . ," and you say, "That's one." If Tommy continues to whine and plead, "That's two" (no more explanation and no further discussion). If Tommy continues and you reach "three," there is a predetermined consequence, such as a ten-minute time-out or an evening without television. Tommy needs to know the consequence ahead of time, and it needs to be appropriate for his age. Phelan stresses the importance of staying calm and not engaging the child in a debate or an argument, thereby avoiding a power struggle. While Glasser's rationale in staying low-key is to avoid becoming *entertainment* for your child, Phelan comes from a slightly different point of view. He feels that because children are little people and feel less powerful than adults, they have a tendency to exert power when they can, and often unpleasantly. Therefore, the ability to push your buttons and get you to react gives the child a gratifying sense of *power*. When this is rewarded by an unsuspecting adult, the child's behavior is far more likely to be repeated.

The ADHD experts tell us that there is slowed brainwave activity in the frontal lobes of ADHD kids (Amen, 2001; Barkley, 1998). A byproduct of this underactivity is a craving for stimulation. The ADHD child wants to see and hear us intensely react. This may at least partially explain the reason kids labeled ADHD often seek out fast-paced, quick-to-respond, even risk-taking behaviors. It may be that it's a subconscious attempt to "fire-up" their otherwise underactive frontal lobes. Therefore, it becomes critical that we react intensely to the appropriate behaviors and react with little emotion to the problem behavior. This reinforces only the desired behavior. In response to problem behavior, a simple, unemotional verbal response will do, along with a swift and appropriate consequence.

Realizing the "energy problem" of the ADHD child and recognizing that his or her need to be stimulated is likely to take priority over *your* need for him to pay attention, consider this. It may be *your* need for your child to pay attention only to you or the task you'd like for him to be focusing on, but not *his* need. You may recall Gabriel from Chapter 4. My need, before I knew better, was for him to leave my wad of keys alone and pay strict attention to what I wanted him to accomplish in the counseling session. It wasn't until I allowed him to hold and rattle around my keys that he began to truly make use of the sessions at all. Remember, your brain (assuming you haven't been labeled ADHD yourself) works differently than your ADHD child's brain. It may make perfect sense to you that your child will learn better if he has nothing else to focus on, but that reasoning may be off the mark. The ADHD-labeled child may actually better absorb what it is you (the parent, teacher, or counselor) want for him or her to absorb, if being allowed to meet his need for greater stimulation at the same time.

Consider allowing your child to rock in a rocking chair while doing homework. The energy required to make the chair move is likely to vent excess energy, allowing the child to pay better attention to the task at hand. At the same time, the rocking motion will most likely be soothing. Consider allowing your child to bounce on a trampoline while encouraging him to talk with you about his day or while discussing a schedule for the week ahead. Your child will be less likely to feel the need to scan for extra stimulation, thereby being distracted from your conversation, if he's bouncing up and down in an energy expending, yet controlled, physical activity. The trampoline should be the small type that can fit easily into a few square feet in a spare room or in the yard. The giant ones that propel a child nearly into the stratosphere may be a little too stimulating, and you will have to wait for your child to come back to earth before you can finish your sentence.

Counselors should consider keeping a jar of fuzzy pipe-cleaners on their desks. Cut in half, they will be the right size for your ADHD-labeled client to hold and mold while in session. The tactile stimulation should help the child better focus on his interaction with you (Williams, 2007).

Teachers should consider allowing your ADHD-labeled students controlled movement while in class. Remember that these kids feel a need to move, hunt, and scan. Using controlled movement as a reward will reinforce appropriate behavior. Consider an arrangement with your student in which he will be allowed to go for a drink of water *after* he's completed the first row of problems in his math packet. Let him know that after completing the second row, he may get up and sharpen his pencil. You'll want to be clear ahead of time that if he has problem along the way, he won't be able to get up again on that day (Williams).

Parents, teachers, and counselors should know it's important to get feedback from your ADHD-labeled kids on what they need to control their behavior. "That didn't work so well today. What do you think we should try tomorrow?" Don't settle for "I don't know" as a response. If necessary, present three ideas to the child and let him pick the one he thinks will be the most helpful. Your kids will be more invested in improving their behavior if they have a sense of partial ownership in the helping process.

Evaluating, Monitoring, and Helping the Whole Child

Over the years, we've encountered many ADHD-labeled children who were having learning and attention problems for a variety of reasons aside from those for which ADHD was responsible. You may recall the old saying, "When you're a hammer, you want to treat everything as if it were a nail." Our culture tends to try to make sense of any undesirable or inappropriate behavior by turning it into a disease or disorder with a specific name. Thirty years ago, who'd ever heard of PMS, erectile dysfunction, or acid reflux disease? We've already recognized that there is a rather heated controversy as to whether the symptoms of ADHD should result in labeling the child as having a disorder. Now, we want to caution you against making sense of the ADHD-labeled child's every unwanted behavior by attributing it to the disorder. More simply put, don't assume that everything an ADHD-labeled child does is because he or she has ADHD. Don't become a hammer in constant search of a nail.

Effectively assessing for ADHD requires input from a number of sources. Figure 7-1 is a diagram of the professionals necessary for an effective evaluation. All sources should provide input to the medical professional, who will ultimately decide whether a diagnosis should be made and medication prescribed.

Teachers and counselors should talk with the child's parents about the child's health and lifestyle. The overall health of the child needs to be addressed first. A sick child won't pay attention, won't behave to your standards, and won't learn effectively. Does he have any chronic health problems, such as asthma, juvenile diabetes, or chronic ear infections? When did he last see a pediatrician? If it's been a while, encourage the parent to make an appointment. This is particularly important if the child's behavior or ability to pay attention has deteriorated suddenly.

Does the child appear to be properly nourished? If a child's brain isn't getting adequate nutrition, it won't do its job. It's a mistake to as-

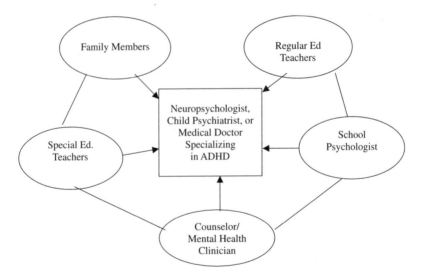

Figure 7-1. Specialists who should have input in a child's evaluation when ADHD is suspected

sume that if a child's weight appears to be in the normal range, he must be properly nourished. It may be that the child is eating mostly empty calories or that his diet is severely lacking in protein.

Is the child getting adequate rest? How many hours sleep is he getting? Does he sleep through the night? Frank was once called to evaluate a 14-year-old Native American/Latina girl who had told her teacher that she was planning to kill herself by taking a whole bottle of her father's seizure medication. During the interview, Luisa told Frank that her mother left the family a year prior, and her father expected her to take on her mother's role as well as to attend and do well in school. For a year, Luisa had been getting up at 5:00 AM each morning so she could make her three younger siblings breakfast and get them dressed for school. In the evening, she was required to cook dinner and clean the dishes. She was responsible for all of the housework throughout the week, including the heavy cleaning. Luisa was overwhelmed and exhausted. She firmly believed that to complain to her father would have been shameful, and she saw suicide as her only option.

Psychosocial stressors in a child's life often result in behavior problems that look like symptoms of a disorder, including ADHD. A child who can't think of anything but the fact that his dad has gone to jail will pay little attention in class. He's likely to be restless, distracted, and irritable, and he may be unable or unwilling to put his worries into words. Furthermore, he may be lacking in the supports he'll need to deal with the stress he is feeling.

Case in Point

Frank was referred a bright, 12-year-old seventh grader because she was anxious and underweight. The suspicion was that she was anorexic. Her teacher made clear that the girl's mother wasn't particularly interested in her daughter receiving counseling, but she would sign the required papers because the school seemed to think counseling would help. Neither was she willing to come to the school to meet with Frank, so the papers were sent home with Marla. Frank managed to interview Marla's mother on the telephone. She described her daughter as a smart and conscientious girl who was strong willed and tended to try and make the decisions for the family. The family consisted of Marla, four younger siblings, and their mother. Marla's biological father was in prison on a drug-related conviction and was to be deported to Mexico after serving his sentence. Marla's mother was unemployed and relied on welfare. Marla's 11-year-old sister was learning handicapped, possibly because of brain trauma received while still in the womb, a victim of her father's domestic violence toward her mother.

It was apparent in the first session that Marla indeed saw it as her responsibility to look out for her brothers and sisters. She made clear that her mother, while well meaning, made one bad decision after another, particularly where men were concerned. Marla saw herself as the protector and primary caregiver of her four siblings. In the sessions that followed, Marla expressed her worry over her siblings, her mother, and even her female cousins who were already sexually active in their early teens. She spoke about her many attempts to talk sense into the people around her, but to no avail. Marla cried and sighed as she spoke, the weight upon her as evident as if she were trying to hold up a house. In a sense, she was doing exactly that. As for her being underweight, it was soon clear that Marla's family relied mainly on government commodities, a box of groceries provided once weekly to disadvantaged families. Forever putting her siblings needs before her own, she was sure to be the last in the family to eat. Marla saw herself as the only person in her life with the judgment necessary to hold things together. For hours, in sessions over several weeks, she was allowed to vent her fears and frustrations, and they were many.

She confided that because her mother had testified against him, her father had made clear his intent to kill the entire family when released from prison. She worried that despite her efforts, she would be unable to keep her brothers from drugs and gangs or her sisters from teenage pregnancy.

To be on the safe side, Frank weighed Marla at each session. He also observed her at lunch on a few occasions. Marla's weight remained constant, never falling below the percentage of normal required to be diagnosed with anorexia nervosa. And her appetite during lunch was nothing less than ravenous. She would eat everything on her tray without hesitation and without the ritual or manipulation of food that's common in people with anorexia. She didn't consider herself fat, as is generally necessary before a diagnosis of anorexia nervosa can be made. Marla's weight issue and anxiety were easily explained. Had Frank been a hammer looking for a nail, he might have come to a different conclusion.

In the small rural system where Frank and Lynn Ann taught and counseled, they had the ability to bring the numerous service-providers together to discuss the issues of children identified as "at risk." Names could be added to the list of kids by any of the providers, including officials from child protective services, schools, the probation department, public health services, and the health clinic. The members of the team may vary depending on the services providers available and willing to participate. A representative from mental health attends the monthly multidisciplinary team (MDT) meeting as well, but because of state and federal confidentiality laws, mental health is there primarily to listen and to provide guidance and information to the other team members. Even though every participant is required to sign a confidentiality oath before attending, discussing clients on the mental health caseload would likely result in a breach of confidentiality.

Not every child labeled ADHD is, or should be, identified as "at risk" and added to the MDT roster. However, if there is a pattern of behavior problems over time, particularly if initial remedies have been unsuccessful or the underlying cause of the behavior is unexplained, a multidisciplinary approach is indicated. A multidisciplinary team generally meets on a monthly basis. One member is usually responsible for leading the meeting, keeping the roster, and distributing the minutes. The meeting is generally held within the county's social services or health and human services office.

The goal of each meeting should be to identify the child at risk, share relevant information regarding the child and family (within the confines of state and federal confidentiality laws), and devise a plan for helping. Before moving down the list to the next child, the entire team should understand what action(s) will be taken before the next meeting and by whom. Progress in assisting the child should be evaluated in the following meeting. The process is repeated from meeting to meeting.

The team should operate from the perspective that the authors have been hammering home since Chapter 1: respect each child's needs as an individual with unique challenges and strengths, including *learning* strengths. At the same time, the participants should be able to imag-

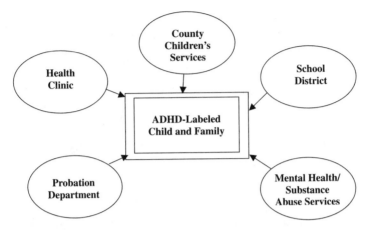

Figure 7-2. A sample multidisciplinary team for supporting the ADHD child

ine themselves in the place of the child and/or family member, who may have very different characteristics (including learning strengths) from their own. Frank and Lynn Ann have seen people fail, almost entirely as a result of the label they were forced to drag behind them like a ball and chain as they trudged through "the system." Even though this book has relied on labels for the purpose of understanding particular similarities in conditions, team members working with kids should avoid labeling whenever possible. That is unless, of course, it is to label each child "unique," a label that applies to every one of us! Every team, which should include the child and his or her parents whenever possible, should strive to understand and arrange for the individual needs of every child it serves, in a spirit of cooperation and in an atmosphere of empathic professionalism.

Kids labeled ADHD and those with other frontal lobe problems that contribute to behavior and learning problems should be able to look to us to help them channel their individual strengths, celebrate their talents, and eventually prepare them for work that will benefit them, their families, and all of society. Properly identified and put to good use, these talented individuals can overcome seemingly insurmountable challenges! Never underestimate the power these kids possess, and never allow them to give up!

Figure 7-1 illustrated those people in a child's life who should provide input to the medical doctor before an ADHD diagnosis is made.

Figure 7-2 illustrated the members of a county's multidisciplinary team, which identifies kids at risk and provides "service-provider" interventions to these kids and their families, and tracks child/family progress.

Figure 7-3 illustrates multimodal interventions for kids diagnosed with ADHD. Each component is essential for meeting the biological, educational, social, and psychological needs of the child and family, supporting the child toward becoming a happy, healthy, and productive adult.

Proper diet is an essential element in managing the biological issues that contribute to ADHD symptoms, including energy management, distractibility, impulsivity, irritability, and mood. Therefore, advise parents to do the following:

1. Allow your child to eat at least three times per day. In fact, five smaller portions per day are even better. This allows for consistent nutrition and lessens the likelihood of blood sugar fluctuation that can cause mood and energy problems.
2. Be sure your child is getting enough iron. Green leafy vegetables are a great source, as is lean meat. If there's doubt, supplements can seal the deal.
3. Limit sugar intake to less than 15 percent of total daily caloric intake and remember the simple carbohydrates, such as those

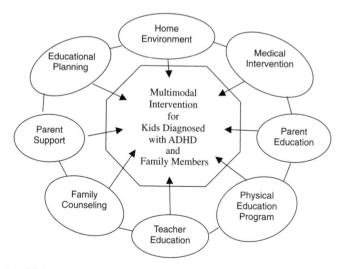

Figure 7-3. Multimodal intervention for children with ADHD

contained in white bread and fructose (fruit sugar), break down to sugar as well. Sugar will significantly contribute to energy and attention problems.

4. Caffeine can actually affect the ADHD brain in much the same way as ADHD medications, such as Ritalin and Adderall. But don't be fooled into thinking that a can of caffeinated soda is a good idea. Caffeine restricts blood flow to the brain and is likely to worsen ADHD symptoms over time (Amen, 2001). Also, the indiscriminate and irregular introduction of a stimulant like caffeine into the equation can make "energy management" more complicated. In comparison to a cup of coffee, which may contain 100 to 200 milligrams of caffeine, a can of regular caffeinated soda usually contains only about 25 milligrams. But the kicker is that when you factor in body weight, a child consuming a regular can of soda is likely to be taking in the caffeine equivalent found in four cups of coffee (Market Watch, 2007).

5. Food additives, particularly artificial coloring and flavor preservatives, are a problem and should be eliminated.

6. It's a good idea to consult with a pediatrician to rule out food allergies that may contribute to mood, energy, and behavior problems. There may be a specific allergy to wheat, dairy products, eggs, peanuts, soy, or fish.

7. Be aware that exposure to lead can be a contributing factor. Lead can be hidden in tap water, paint, poorly soldered metal cans, pottery, and glazes.

A particularly helpful tool for gaining insight into the relationship between diet and behavior problems in ADHD-labeled kids is to closely monitor your child's diet, medicines, and supplements, while at the same time tracking behavior, energy, and attention. Record dates and times as you go, and what will emerge can help pinpoint dietary issues that may be causing ADHD-like symptoms or exacerbating actual symptoms.

Lastly, do what you can to obtain effective communication with the doctor who might be prescribing medication to your child, and the parent who is seeing that the child is taking it (assuming that's not you). Oftentimes, ADHD medications are managed on a trial-and-error basis, at least initially, and changes in behavior and attention may be medication related. Without knowing for certain if a medication or dosage change has been made, your team will be flying blind.

The chapter closes with some very specific considerations that Frank and Lynn Ann have found vital in working with ADHD-labeled kids. Some will be relevant to some kids and not others, so know the children you're working with and carry out the suggestions that will benefit the individual child. These suggestions are likely to have a very positive effect on your child's physical, mental, or emotional preparedness, enhancing their ability to attend to tasks. Remember to expect inconsistency, so much a part of the lives and temperaments of the kids you're determined to help. Something might seem to work like a magic pill one day, in a specific situation, then flop miserably on another day in a different or even the same situation.

- Minimize noise, bright lights, and excessive activity by others around the child. Find out what bothers the child (certain types of clothing, room temperature, etc.).
- Put the child close to you, and use eye contact and physical contact (light touch on the shoulder) to keep his/her attention when speaking or demonstrating.
- Give the child frequent breaks for PHYSICAL ACTIVITY.
- Help manage behavior by using SIMPLE and SPECIFIC RULES. Be sure the child understands the consequences.
- PRAISE the child often for good behavior and use rewards immediately, whenever possible.
- Give directions ONE AT A TIME.
- Stay calm and BE CONSISTENT with consequences. Consider giving the child a "time-out" and then discuss inappropriate behaviors.
- Help the child's self esteem by spending special time with him/her.
- Use nonverbal cues to help him/her stay on task.
- Try to plan things earlier in the day and stick to a ROUTINE as much as possible.
- Allow time for the child to digest information. If you've asked a question, wait patiently for an answer, whenever possible.
- Let the child know ahead of time when changing activities.

- Help him/her ORGANIZE by using visual cues such as assignment sheets, "To Do" lists, or reminders using symbols or graphics.
- Use CONTRACTS to help develop good behavior or work habits. Use rewards that the child enjoys and teach him/her how to reward themselves for "a job well done."
- Discuss learning styles, CELEBRATE THE CHILD'S STRENGTHS, and teach him/her how to compensate.

8

Getting Started

The materials in Appendixes I and II are fun and simple to use. You will find detailed instructions in this chapter.

Appendix I contains the survey and scoring materials, as well as the Seven Pillars graph. These materials help you determine your child's favored learning styles.

Appendix II contains the 42 "brain exercising" activities designed to teach your child to manage his or her behavior, anticipate consequences and the actions of others, and to improve his or her situational awareness.

The scores obtained from using the materials in Appendix I will determine which activities in Appendix II are best for your child, depending on his or her strongest learning strengths and favored learning styles. Using the activities that correspond with your child's weaker learning styles creates the opportunity for further developing strength in these learning styles.

Using the Learning Style Survey
(in Appendix I)

The 56-question survey (Appendix I) is to aide you, the "helper" (parent, teacher, or counselor), to determine the child's individual learning strengths. In completing the survey, the child enters a 1, 2, or 3 for each question. A "1" indicates the answer is never, a "2" means sometimes, and a "3" means always. There are eight questions corresponding to each of the learning styles.

We strongly encourage you to allow the child to complete the survey independently whenever possible, but it's perfectly acceptable to read the questions aloud to younger kids and those with learning handicaps. It's also perfectly fine to clarify questions for the child whenever necessary.

Scoring

To score the survey, simply enter the child's numeric answer (1, 2, or 3) for each question above the corresponding question number on the scoring sheet. Then total the values for each of the seven learning styles.

Graphing

For a more visual take on the survey results, encourage your child to enter the scores on the Seven Pillars Graph by coloring in the totaled values in the corresponding seven columns. The more colorful the better for stimulating those frontal lobes and getting your child interested in his individual learning strengths. This knowledge can serve him or her over and over throughout a lifetime.

Consider completing the survey for yourself and coloring in a Seven Pillars Graph of your own. It can be fun and interesting for the child and helper to compare their individual results. Doing so serves as a valuable lesson to the child that learning strengths vary by individual, and one isn't better than the other, just different. Besides, by now you're going to be curious about how you learn best!

The survey is a compilation of the authors' many years of experience working with children and drawing on the works of leaders in the field, including Thomas Armstrong and David Lazear. We specifically designed our survey to be a good fit with the activities. Our survey is not normed, and we don't intend to represent it to be a psychometric test. In fact, if you're interested in checking out some other quality surveys, have a look on the internet at LD.Pride.net, Learning-Styles-online.com, and Advanogy.com.

Using the Activities (in Appendix II)

Pairing Survey Findings with the Activities

Scoring the completed survey and coloring in the graph in Appendix I will result in an individual child profile. The profile will give the reader insight into the learning strengths of the child, or, simply put, how the child learns best. Now these results can be paired with the activities in Appendix II. For example, if the scoring indicates that the child may be a strong verbal-linguistic learner, the reader might choose the activities in section G of Appendix II. If the survey scoring indicates the same child's second greatest learning style is bodily-kinesthetic, then the reader may choose to use the activities in section B. The helper might want to then move on to the child's third greatest style, and so on. Focusing on the activities identified as being the child's weaker learning styles may prove a useful opportunity for helping your child to better develop these styles.

Thinking, Feeling, Doing: A Delicate Interplay

Behavior problems are not simply a result of "bad behavior." Behavior, appropriate or inappropriate, doesn't happen in a vacuum. What we "do" (behavior) is largely a result of what we "think" (cognition) and how we "feel" (emotion). Therefore, we've divided the activities (brain exercises) into thinking, feeling, and doing, to address all three of the elements that contribute to behavior.

To All Readers

The activities frequently call for discussion or play between you and the child. Such interaction allows for learning far beyond the activity itself. We strongly encourage you to develop the topic featured in the activity in a manner appropriate for the individual child. Never underestimate the importance of the quality of the interaction between "helper" and child. Patience, a caring attitude, and active listening are essential to the process.

Freeman, Epston, and Lobovitz state in their work *Playful Approaches to Serious Problems* (1997), "When we stay curious and open, our faith is rewarded by the mutual creativity that is generated in our relationship with children."

Consider allowing your child the use of a pipe cleaner, trampoline, or rocking chair while working on the activities with you. If you're really confused by the last sentence, you didn't read Chapter 7. We certainly wouldn't want you to throw in the towel before you've even gotten started, so we'll summarize here. Expecting your child's full attention when first using the activities might be unrealistic and frustrating. If the activity allows for it, let your child hold and mold a fuzzy pipe cleaner, rock in a rocking chair, or even bounce on a small trampoline. The need to be scanning the environment for more stimulation should be quieted by one of these controlled, self-soothing strategies, while working on the activity at the same time.

Don't settle for "I don't know" responses from your child while working at the activities. Set this as a ground rule before you get started. Your gut will tell you whether your child truly can't come up with an answer to your question, is playing it safe, or is resisting the process entirely. But in most cases, a child can come up with some kind of answer that will lead to further discussion and eventual discovery. In response to "I don't know," patiently remind your child that the term is off limits and ask for their best guess. If they still seem at a loss, have them choose from three possible answers that you supply. Then when they do, get excited about their answer and praise them up and down for coming out from behind "I don't know."

Summary

The 42 activities contained here will not "cure" ADHD, but we're confident that repeatedly emphasizing these themes every day (dragging your child over to his or her frontal lobe, figuratively speaking) will have positive results similar to those obtained with our kids. These themes include empathy, correctly identifying the intentions of others, anticipating consequences, identifying feelings, normalizing emotions, seeing the big picture, choosing alternative behaviors, learning from competent role models, positive affirmations, self-monitoring, relaxation training, and thought stopping.

That's all there is to it. You now have everything you need to get started. Remember to make the activity time quality time for all!

Examples That Demonstrate Use of Interventions

Black-and-White Belinda

Tony is a ten-year-old fifth grader who has a tendency to get down on himself. When he does, he is a negative thinker who tends to believe the worst about every situation. Tony comes home from school in a bad mood because on the bus ride home, the driver called out on the loudspeaker for Tony to sit down in his seat, embarrassing him in front of the other kids.

> Tony: "He's always yelling at me."
> "That guy hates me."
> "Everybody gets up off the seat."
> "I'll never ride on his bus again."

After allowing Tony to present his side of the story and vent his frustration, the helper might want to talk to Tony about black-and-white thinking and work with Tony on the activity titled "Black-and-White Belinda." After completing the activity, consider taking each of Tony's statements (listed above) and asking Tony if he has been thinking in black and white. Ask Tony to come up with some more realistic thoughts about the situation on his own. If he can't (or won't), consider offering up a few of your own thoughts for Tony to consider, such as:

> "You said that the bus driver is always yelling at you. Do you remember him ever yelling at anyone else to sit down?"
> "You said the bus driver hates you. Can you think of another reason that he might tell you to sit down in your seat?"
> "Could he be trying to keep you from getting hurt?"
> "You said that everyone gets up off the seat. That must make the driver's job of keeping everyone safe very hard. Do you think that might make him a little stressed and grumpy?"
> "You said that you'll never ride that bus again. Have you thought about how you'll get to school without riding the bus?"

Friends or Foes

Sylvia is a bright nine-year-old fourth grader who is feeling like an outsider since her best friend Tina has been paying attention to a new student in their class. Sylvia has become irritable and sullen.

> "Tina doesn't like me anymore."
> "I don't ever want to play with Tina again."
> "I hate that new girl."

After patiently allowing Sylvia to express her feelings about the situation, the helper might want to introduce Sylvia to the activity titled "Friends or Foes." After completing the activity, consider asking Sylvia if maybe Tina likes both her and the new girl.

"Is Tina your enemy just because she has another friend besides you?"

"Has the new girl done anything to make you think she doesn't like you, too?"

"How about asking both Tina and the new girl over for pizza and a movie on Saturday?"

Cool Like Who

Jeff is a 12-year-old sixth grader, who has a tough time waiting his turn. He seems unable to keep from trying to work his way to the front of any line, blurting out an answer in class without raising his hand, or allowing others at the dinner table to take their portions before grabbing the goods. The helper may want to bring this behavior to Jeff's attention. Allow Jeff to give you examples of how this has been a problem for him.

"My teacher put my name on the board twice this week."

"There's a big kid in the cafeteria who told me I better not ever take cuts in front of him."

The helper should suggest they work together to solve the problem.

"What are some ways we can try to help you wait your turn?"

Make Jeff's ideas part of an overall plan.

Introduce Jeff to the activity titled "Cool Like Who?" Ask Jeff to think of someone "cool" in his life. Someone he respects and looks up to. Maybe he'll come up with his dad, his P.E. Coach, or a TV character. Maybe even a superhero like Spiderman. Now ask Jeff to imagine his cool character in some of those situations where Jeff gets impulsive.

"What do you picture your dad doing while he's in line at the cafeteria?"

"Would he be trying to cut ahead?" "Maybe he'd be talking to his friend about their plans for Saturday, to help pass the time in line."

Remember, it's always best if Jeff can come up with his own solutions, so be sure and give him a chance.

"Would your coach be grabbing at the food on the table when someone is trying to take their share?"

"Do you think maybe he would make sure his little sister got her share first?"

X Marks the Spot

Celia is a nine-year-old fourth grader who easily gets irritated, especially when her teacher or her mother tells her to settle down and pay attention. She's heard those words so many times, they make her want to scream, and sometimes she does. The helper might want to help Celia learn to pay attention to how her body feels when she first starts to get irritated, and before she's beyond the point of no return. Help Celia with the activity titled "X Marks the Spot."

Asking Celia to notice and talk about the things her body is trying to tell her will make it much easier for her to redirect her anger before it's too late. Be sure and ask questions that will help Celia notice the things that will be most helpful to her.

"When you first start to get irritated, where in your body do you feel it?"

"And what does it feel like?"

"What do you think you could do when you notice it starting again so that you can stay in control?"

If Celia can't come up with ideas on her own, give her some strategies to choose from.

"Suppose when you first notice that hot feeling in your stomach you take three great big breaths?"

"How about squeezing and relaxing your fists ten times in a row and counting to ten at the same time?"

"Maybe when you notice that hot feeling in your stomach, you could pull out the picture of Molly (Celia's puppy) that you carry in your pocket and think about how much fun you have throwing the ball for her."

"Which of those three ideas are you going to try first?"

It's important to remind Celia that like learning anything new, it takes practice. Celia shouldn't expect perfection on the first try.

"Let's talk about it again in a couple of days and see how it went. If those ideas didn't do the trick, we can work on doing them better. And we can always think up some new ideas together."

Using the Activities

Make the activities fun to use. Be creative. Take your child well beyond the simple activity on the page in a way that makes the activity specific to your child's needs.

It's best to use the activities at a time when you're feeling well rested and relaxed. Most importantly of all, do your best to be patient and nurturing for your child. There's nothing more healing for a child than feeling the love and concern of a caring adult.

Once you've had a chance to participate in the activities with your child, perhaps you would be interested in sharing your thoughts. The authors would greatly appreciate your feedback, particularly about what was useful and what was not so useful. We promise to use your insights in creating the second edition. You can reach the authors via email at frankjac@hotmail.com or lawatson@clearwire.net.

Survey of the Seven Strengths

Please read the statements carefully and mark each one with a score of 1 to 3 (1 never, 2 sometimes, and 3 always).

1. _____ I like and remember more information from listening to radio, CDs, or lectures than watching a film or television.

2. _____ I feel more comfortable visualizing or drawing the steps in a problem rather than trying to figure it out in my head.

3. _____ Sports and/or physical activities are more fun for me than activities that require sitting for long periods of time.

4. _____ I like listening to music a lot.

5. _____ People seem to come to me for advice or help.

6. _____ I like math and/or science more than literature and history.

7. _____ I would rather spend time alone than with a crowd.

8. _____ I like to play games that are active, like charades or tag, more than putting together jigsaw puzzles or playing word games.

9. _____ I like making people laugh and I remember puns and jokes easily.

10. _____ I like drawing and illustrating rather than writing or speaking.

11. _____ I like working in groups of people.

12. _____ I like to find solutions to brainteasers, pattern games, and puzzles.

13. _____ I have hobbies or interests that I don't necessarily share with others.

14. _____ I love to sing, hum, and/or play musical instruments.

15. _____ I enjoy team sports or games like charades rather than solitary games that I play alone or with one other person.

16. _____ I like to question theories and experiment with hypotheses.

17. _____ I enjoy acting and dancing more than reading and math.

18. _____ I love to verbally debate with others more than getting involved in physical competition.

19. _____ I remember information easier if it has a beat or tune to it.

20. _____ I would rather use the videocamera than a tape recorder.

21. _____ I have goals and aspirations that I feel are important to work on often.

22. _____ I would rather spend my free time outdoors.

23. _____ I love photographs and books with lots of illustrations.

24. _____ I get involved in social activities frequently (clubs, sports, groups).

25. _____ I can figure out answers to mathematical problems in my head easily.

26. _____ I can write my own music and/or create musical patterns.

27. _____ I like spending time with myself and/or enjoy learning about personal growth.

28. _____ Words are really important to me so I really enjoy reading books and/or poetry.

29. _____ I like to figure out what makes things work and I can invent ways to improve them.

30. _____ I have many friends and more than two that I would call "close friends."

31. _____ I spend time reflecting on important life questions and/or issues.

32. _____ I enjoy using vocabulary words that others don't understand sometimes.

33. _____ I find myself whistling, humming, or singing often.

34. _____ Colors can affect my moods and I like to coordinate them.

35. _____ I have trouble sitting for long periods of time.

36. _____ When I have something to work out, I feel more comfortable talking about it with friends rather than trying to work it out myself.

37. _____ After hearing a song or tune once or twice, I can usually play it, hum it, or sing it well.

38. _____ I can spend hours concentrating on something that is important to me.

39. _____ I remember people's faces better than their names.

40. _____ After learning something new, I would rather practice it myself than watch someone else do it.

41. _____ The subjects in school that are easier for me are literature, social studies, and history.

42. _____ I can easily see how others could organize their daily activities in a logical way that would utilize time more efficiently.

43. _____ I enjoy finding patterns or sequences in the things I see or do (patterns of nature or the steps in the construction of a building).

44. _____ I often have views that are different from the rest of the "crowd."

45. _____ I am the type of person who uses body language when I am speaking to someone else.

46. _____ Others see me as a leader.

47. _____ I can keep the beat to music easily.

48. _____ I have vivid dreams and can see pictures easily in my head.

49. _____ I enjoy games that use words like crosswords.

50. _____ I like it when things are organized in some way.

51. _____ My best ideas happen while I am doing some sort of physical activity.

52. _____ I would like to work alone or have my own business some day.

53. _____ I can use music to express my feelings and music sometimes affects my mood.

54. _____ I love to use my imagination.

55. _____ I would rather be at a concert or popular sports event than home alone.

56. _____ I do well on vocabulary quizzes and written essays.

To score your questionnaire, follow these basic steps. After each Strength Heading, write each score from the survey above the question number, then add the scores to get the grand total. Take each of the totals and graph them on the Seven Strengths Graph. You may color in each column to be able to "see" which may be your best learning styles. Using this information, you and your helper may choose the activity sections that utilize your strengths to help you deal with a particular situation.

Logical-Mathematical

$$\frac{\quad}{6} + \frac{\quad}{12} + \frac{\quad}{16} + \frac{\quad}{25} + \frac{\quad}{29} + \frac{\quad}{42} + \frac{\quad}{43} + \frac{\quad}{50} = \underline{\quad}$$

Bodily-Kinesthetic

$$\frac{\quad}{3} + \frac{\quad}{8} + \frac{\quad}{17} + \frac{\quad}{22} + \frac{\quad}{35} + \frac{\quad}{40} + \frac{\quad}{45} + \frac{\quad}{51} = \underline{\quad}$$

Intrapersonal

$$\frac{\quad}{7} + \frac{\quad}{13} + \frac{\quad}{21} + \frac{\quad}{27} + \frac{\quad}{31} + \frac{\quad}{38} + \frac{\quad}{44} + \frac{\quad}{52} = \underline{\quad}$$

Musical-Rhythmic

$$\frac{\quad}{4} + \frac{\quad}{14} + \frac{\quad}{19} + \frac{\quad}{26} + \frac{\quad}{33} + \frac{\quad}{37} + \frac{\quad}{47} + \frac{\quad}{53} = \underline{\quad}$$

Visual-Spatial

$$\frac{\quad}{2} + \frac{\quad}{10} + \frac{\quad}{20} + \frac{\quad}{23} + \frac{\quad}{34} + \frac{\quad}{39} + \frac{\quad}{48} + \frac{\quad}{54} = \underline{\quad}$$

Interpersonal

$$\frac{\quad}{5} + \frac{\quad}{11} + \frac{\quad}{15} + \frac{\quad}{24} + \frac{\quad}{30} + \frac{\quad}{36} + \frac{\quad}{46} + \frac{\quad}{55} = \underline{\quad}$$

Verbal-Linguistic

$$\frac{\quad}{1} + \frac{\quad}{9} + \frac{\quad}{18} + \frac{\quad}{28} + \frac{\quad}{32} + \frac{\quad}{41} + \frac{\quad}{49} + \frac{\quad}{56} = \underline{\quad}$$

7 STRENGTHS GRAPH

	Logical Mathematical	Bodily Kinesthetic	Intrapersonal	Musical Rhythmic	Visual Spatial	Interpersonal	Verbal Linguistic
24							
23							
22							
21							
20							
19							
18							
17							
16							
15							
14							
13							
12							
11							
10							
9							
8							
7							
6							
5							
4							
3							
2							
1							

"Brain-Exercising" Activities

WORKBOOK A

Logical-Mathematical Activities

A-1   THIS THING CALLED ADHD

Time required: 15 minutes
Materials required: Pencil or marker
*This is a **thinking** activity*

Everybody's brain works a little differently! Some people's brains work in a way that causes a condition called attention-deficit hyperactivity disorder . . . ADHD for short.

If you have ADHD then this book is about helping you to overcome some of the problems that ADHD can cause in your life. Things like having trouble paying attention for very long (unless the subject is something new and interesting. Then you have no trouble at all, I'll bet!), sitting still, getting angry or irritable more times than you'd like, and maybe getting in trouble more than most kids. Maybe sometimes your thinking seems a little fuzzy and you just don't know why. Well, in case you didn't know it, you're not dumb, lazy, or bad. Maybe you just have a brain that works a little differently. Maybe you have ADHD.

And here's some more good news. There are things that you can learn to do to help you overcome the problems that ADHD can cause. That's what this book is all about. Want one more piece of good news? Someone cares about you so much that they went out and got this book for you to have fun with . . . and learn from.

Did you know that some pretty amazing people have (or had) ADHD? People like **Walt Disney, Galileo, Robin Williams, Henry Ford, and John Lennon** (just to name a few) (Low, 2007). Maybe you've heard of them?

Just for fun, match the person's name on the left with the picture of the thing on the right that made them famous.

Walt Disney

Galileo

Henry Ford

Robin Williams

John Lennon

If you have ADHD, you're in pretty good company!

A-2   FUMING FREDDIE

Time required: 20–40 minutes
Materials required: worksheet, marker or pencil
*This is a **thinking** activity*

Freddie gets in trouble all the time because of his temper. He loses his cool almost every day. Freddie's friends get disappointed when Freddie gets mad because he loses his privileges and he can't spend time with them doing the things they all like, like riding bikes, roller-blading and playing computer games. **Freddie's friends can't figure out why Freddie gets so mad over little things.**

One day while Freddie and his friends were in class and learning about science, Freddie raised his hand to answer a question about why plants are green. Freddie knew all about the chemical called chlorophyll that makes plants green, and how plants needed sunlight to grow. Freddie loves plants and nature.

When his teacher picked on someone else to answer the question Freddie threw his book across the room, yelled at his teacher, then sat back in his chair, crossed his arms and scowled!

Freddie was in the habit of thinking mad thoughts. What do you suppose were the thoughts in Freddie's head that were causing him to lose his cool? Print those thoughts in Fuming Freddie's thought cloud.

If Freddie was not in the habit of thinking mad thoughts, **what do you suppose he would be thinking after the teacher didn't call on him?** Print these in Cool Freddie's thought cloud.

Do <u>you</u> think mad thoughts or cool thoughts? Which Freddie would you like to be?

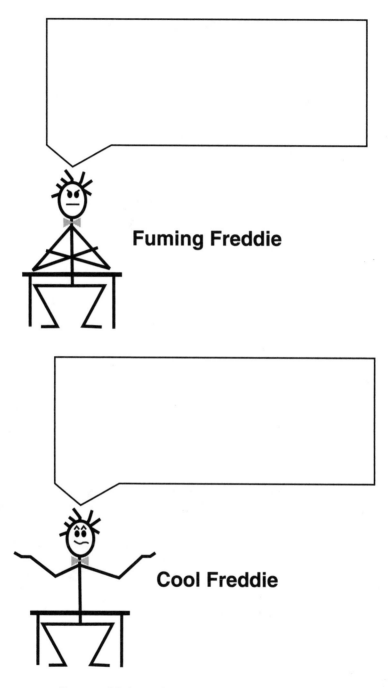

Do you think mad thoughts or cool thoughts?

A-3   WHEN FEELINGS TAKE SHAPE

Time required: 10–20 minutes
Materials required: worksheet, markers or pencil
*This is a **feeling** activity*

Sometimes our feelings come in bunches. Take Kelly for example. She received the highest grade in her class for her science project about dinosaurs. Kelly's teacher has asked her to attend a parent-teacher dinner on Friday night. After everyone has finished eating, Kelly will get up in front of the room with her project and tell everyone about dinosaurs. Kelly can think of five feelings she is having.

A figure with five sides is called a **pentagon.** To help her identify her feelings, Kelly has named each side of a pentagon.

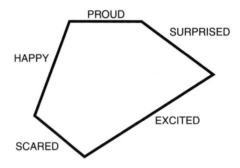

Dwayne is one of the best soccer players on his team, which is playing for the city championship in two days. But today, Dwayne fell off his skateboard and banged his knee. His knee is bruised and swollen, and he can barely walk. Dwayne believes his knee would be okay if he had been wearing kneepads, like his friends do. **What do you suppose Dwayne is feeling?**

A **square** is a figure with four sides. **Dwayne needs some help in naming his feelings.** Think about how Dwayne might be feeling then **name the four sides of the square in your workbook.**

When Feelings Take Shape

Can you help Dwayne name his feelings, and give them **shape**?

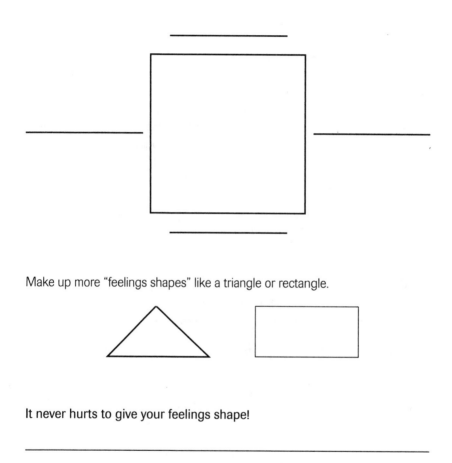

Make up more "feelings shapes" like a triangle or rectangle.

It never hurts to give your feelings shape!

_____

_____

_____

_____

_____

_____

A-4 THE CLASS THAT GASPED

Time required: 20–40 minutes
Materials required: worksheet, pencil
*This is a **feeling** activity*

Mr. Taylor's sixth grade class had been planning a weeklong trip to Washington, D.C. They washed cars, sold cookies, and even mowed lawns on weekends to help pay for the trip. The kids were eager to see the White House, the Capitol, the Lincoln Memorial, and all the other historic landmarks that the nation's capital had to offer.

Then, one Monday morning, Mr. Taylor announced that half of the class had been disqualified from attending the trip because they had been caught with beer at a party on the weekend. The kids in the class were **aghast!**

They got to thinking about their choices! Were they using their brains to think ahead? Were they even thinking about the consequences of getting caught? What other things did they think about?

You can just imagine what the kids must be feeling! Use the clues to complete the puzzle. **Fill in the blanks with the name of the feeling each of the students might be feeling.**

ACROSS

1- Donnie knew better than to go to a party where there was beer, but he went to fit in with his friends. Now he feels _____ .

2- Kate didn't know about the party but her friend Lisa was asked to go. Lisa said no. Kate is _____ of Lisa.

3- Mike was really looking forward to the trip but now he blew it. Mike is feeling _____ .

4- Josh's parents don't know about the beer yet, but they will. Josh is feeling _____ .

DOWN

1- Lisa learned that her best friend Jessie had beer at the party. Lisa couldn't believe it! Lisa is _____ .

2- Robbie almost went to the party but then heard there might be beer and didn't go after all. Now he is _____ .

How do you suppose Mr. Taylor feels?

_____

_____

_____

_____

_____

A-5 GLENN GETS IT DONE

Time required: through the week
Materials required: Markers
*This is a **doing** activity*

Glenn used to have a hard time finishing things: homework, chores, even dinner! His mom came up with an idea to help Glenn stay on track.

Glenn's mom made sure Glenn got a reward for staying on track, and what do you think happened? Glenn learned to Get it Done!

Here's how it works. Glenn and his mom made up a "Task/Reward Table." On a piece of paper, Glenn and his mom made a list of the tasks Glenn was having trouble finishing. Next to that list, they jotted down what Glenn would have to get done in order to get a reward. And next to that was the reward Glenn would get. Glenn's Table looked something like this:

Task	To Get Reward	Reward
1. Homework	three math problems	five minutes on computer
	Finish math	five more minutes on computer
2. Chores	Feed and water Sparky and take out the garbage	15 minutes to play outside before homework
3. Dinner	Eat half-serving of main dish	Can eat half of dessert
	Finish serving of veggies	Can finish dessert

After a few days, Glenn was glad for the "Task/Reward Table." He liked that his mom and dad could stop hounding him about not getting things done. After a little practice, Glenn's mom started pasting gold stars next to each task that Glenn completed. When there were stars by every task for a whole week, Glenn got to pick a weekend reward like going for ice cream, renting a movie, or having a sleepover!

Together with your helper, use this page to start your own "Task/Reward Table." Because, like Glenn, you can learn to Get it Done!

Task	To Get Reward	Reward
1. _____	_____	_____
_____	_____	_____
2. _____	_____	_____
_____	_____	_____
3. _____	_____	_____
_____	_____	_____
4. _____	_____	_____
_____	_____	_____

A star by every task for a week? You can choose from one of these three rewards on the weekend (filled in by mom or dad)!

1. _____

_____

2. _____

_____

3. _____

_____

Can you Get it Done?

A-6 LUKE MAKES A LIST

Time required: 20 minutes
Materials required: markers
*This is a **doing** activity*

Luke is a bright fifth grader who gets off track sometimes. One minute he's working on his chores, and before he knows it, he's playing with his baseball cards or video games. He'd get so wrapped up in having fun, that he'd never get around to finishing things.

Luke wanted to learn to stay on track and not forget. Together with his dad, Luke learned to Make a List. Whenever he would finish his chores, his homework, or whatever he had to, he'd check it off his list.

At the end of the week Luke's list looked like this:

	Sun.	Mon.	Tues.	Wed.	Thu.	Fri.	Sat.
1. Brush Teeth	X	X	X	X	X	X	X
2. Feed and water Fluffy	X	X	X	X	X	X	X
3. Finish Homework	—	X	X	X	X	X	—
4. Get a Hug before Bed	X	X	X	X	X	X	X

When Luke's list looks like this at the end of the week, he gets some extra special time with his dad. Sometimes they go to a movie on Sunday afternoon, or have a picnic at the park.

In the beginning, his dad had to remind Luke to work on his list every day. But after a while, Luke could remember all on his own.

Luke was glad he had a list to help him stay on track, and so was his dad! Use this page to make a list for yourself!

_____ **Makes a List**

	Sun.	Mon.	Tues.	Wed.	Thu.	Fri.	Sat.
1. _____							
2. _____							
3. _____							
4. _____							
5. _____							

_____ **Makes a List**

	Sun.	Mon.	Tues.	Wed.	Thu.	Fri.	Sat.
1. _____							
2. _____							
3. _____							
4. _____							
5. _____							

Remember to put your list where you can see it every day.

Talk to your helper about your reward for making your list look like Luke's!

Bodily-Kinesthetic Activities

B-1 MAKING SCENTS OF THOUGHTS AND FEELINGS

Time required: one-half hour preparation, 20–30-minute activity
Materials required: various spices, extracts, film containers, labels,
*   marker, pencil, worksheet*
*This is a **thinking** activity*

One of the important ways that we experience the world around us is with our sense of smell. We are usually able to quickly tell the difference between a smell we like and one we don't. Some smells can be dangerous, like ammonia, bug spray, and most chemicals. They smell awful, and we quickly know to keep those fumes away. **Wouldn't it be nice to have a sniffer that could warn us when our thoughts are causing us trouble? Or a nose that could help us to better understand our feelings?**

To have some fun with this idea and maybe learn a little about yourself, start by getting your mom or dad's permission, and maybe their help, to smell around in the spice cupboard. Find seven or eight small containers such as film containers, and put a little bit of the smelliest spices into separate containers. Be sure you have lids for the containers so you can keep the smell inside. Some great smells to start with are garlic, onion, cinnamon, curry powder or pepper, whole cloves, vanilla, and lemon extracts. Label the containers with a marker.

When you get together with your helper, take the containers and this worksheet along.

Read the situations and think about how each of them might make you feel. Some examples are HAPPY, SAD, MAD, SCARED, DISGUSTED, SURPRISED, or choose others. Write down the feeling next to the situation, then the name of the container which most smells like the feeling to you. **Use your imagination and have fun!**

	Feeling	Container
You are planning to spend a day at the ocean with your family	_____	_____
Your puppy is sick and has to go to the doctor	_____	_____
You just learned that you scored the highest grade in the class	_____	_____
The bully of the school wants to see you after class	_____	_____
Someone has been spreading a nasty rumor about you	_____	_____
The only things for lunch are snails and prune juice	_____	_____

Use this space for other ideas you might have . . .

_____

_____

_____

_____

_____

_____

_____

B-2 BETTY'S BLACK BOX

Time required: 30–60 minutes
Materials required: box, paint, paintbrush, scissors, cloth, tape, objects
*This is a **thinking** activity*

Betty's auntie has a fun way of **helping Betty to think about some of the important things in her life.** Betty and her auntie started with a cardboard box and made a hole in the side big enough for Betty's hand to pass through. They stapled some black velvet material around the hole to keep the contents secret. Then they colored the box a mysterious black!

Next, Betty's auntie put some interesting small objects into the box when Betty wasn't around. She chose very different things of different shapes and textures. Some were jagged without being sharp, some were rough, and others were smooth as could be. Some were flat while others were round. Some things were thick and heavy, and others were light as a feather.

Betty's
Black Box

Then came the fun part. Betty liked to put her hand inside the box and feel around. She would take her time and notice all the different shapes, sizes, and textures. She would feel the weight of each object and notice how each felt in her hand. The first time Betty went into the box, her auntie had loaded it with a penny, a plump raisin, a small polished stone, a playing card, a fair sized rock, a big metal washer with a hole in the middle, a stretchy rubber band, and even a small pointy plastic fork.

Betty used the black box to learn about feelings, ideas, and even people. Betty could think up anything that had been on her mind, then feel around for the object that most felt like the thing she was thinking about. That first day Betty was worried about her little sister who was in the hospital having an operation. When Betty went looking for an object that most felt like her worry about her sister, she decided on the rock, which was fat and heavy compared to the other objects. Betty held the rock for a long time and told her auntie all about her sister.

On another day Betty chose the cold metal washer with the hole in the middle and told her auntie about an argument she was having with her best friend. She explained that she felt like she too had a hole inside of her. On yet another day Betty chose the smooth round polished stone, just because that day she felt happy inside. Betty's auntie changed the objects in the box now and then, just to keep it interesting.

Make a Black Box with your helper and see what you might learn!

To help you get started, make a list of the objects you'll want to put into your box by drawing the objects in the box below.

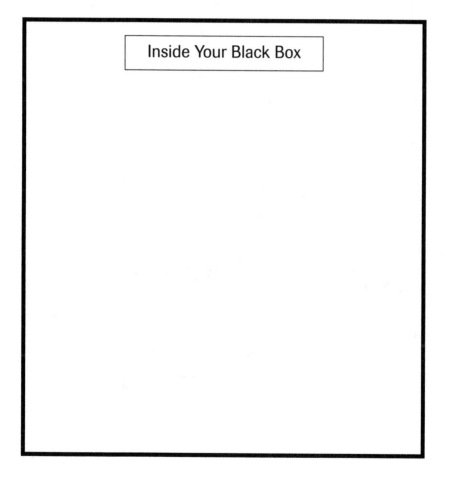

Inside Your Black Box

Now you're ready to make your own black box!

B-3   MAD ME

Time required: 20–30 minutes
Materials required: worksheet, pencil, drawing paper, colored markers
*This is a **feeling** activity*

Our body is good at giving us signals when we are beginning to get angry. Different people get different signals from their bodies. One person might feel their heart begin to pound in their chest, their palms get sweaty, and their hands begin to tremble. Another person might feel their whole body get hot, their stomach start to ache, and their jaw clench shut.

Close your eyes and think about the last time that you began to get very angry. **What signals did your body give you?**

Learning about body signals is important because once you know about them you can pay attention the next time you begin to get angry, and then do something to stop your anger from getting the best of you.

Use the "Mad Me" in your workbook to mark the parts where your signals come from.

Next, **color in the parts where your signals come from.** Use any colors that feel right for showing your anger signals.

Now talk to your helper about your drawing and the signals your body gives you.

There are lots of things you can do when you first notice your body's anger signals to stop the anger from growing, and it's never too late to learn about them. Your helper can teach you what to do when you first notice your body becoming angry.

Create yourself.
Then color in the parts where your anger signals come from.

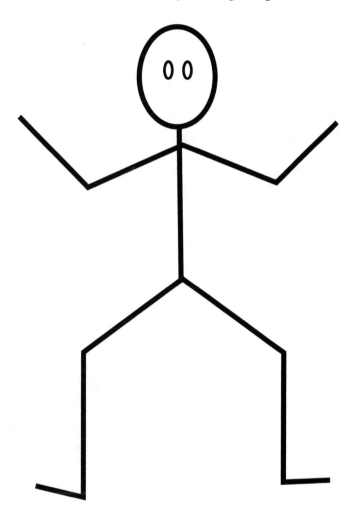

What do your anger signals feel like?

_____

_____

_____

_____

B-4   TOO TIGHT TO FIGHT

Time required: 10–15 minutes
Materials required: worksheet
*This is a **feeling** activity*

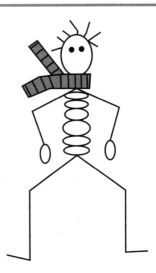

If you like to shoot baskets, play a musical instrument, hit a baseball, or learn your multiplication tables, you know that all these things get easier with **practice.** The same is true for learning to relax.

As funny as it sounds, tensing up the muscles in your body can help you stay calm and relaxed. It just takes a little practice. Follow the steps below, along with your helper. Before you know it, you will be **too tight to fight.**

First, get yourself into a comfortable position. Seated in a comfortable chair is best. Have your feet on the floor and don't cross your arms or legs. You can keep your eyes open or closed. Just think about how your body feels. Think of nothing else for now.

Start by tightening the muscles in your feet and legs, as tight as you can—even curl your toes. Hold this tension in your muscles and count slowly to ten. Hold it! Now relax those muscles all at once. Let all that tension go. Take a few seconds and notice how relaxed your legs and feet feel.

Now, concentrate on your stomach and chest. You got it. Tighten those muscles as tight as you can. Hold it! Count to ten . . . and relax! Let *all* the tension go. Notice the relaxed feeling in your chest and tummy.

Now think about your shoulders and arms. Tighten up! Hold it! Count slowly to ten. . . . Now relax.

Now pay attention to your whole body at once. Notice any tension left in any of your muscles? If so, let it drift away. Notice how relaxed your whole body feels. Feels good, huh?

Talk with your helper about how and when to use this **too tight to fight** helper. And, don't forget to practice!

Get ready to relax!

Take a seat in a comfortable chair.
Take a few deep breaths and relax
your body.

Close your eyes or leave them open,
it's up to you.

Now listen to your helper's voice and
practice . . .

RELAXING!

Later, make a list of the parts of your body that felt the tightest.

_____

_____

_____

_____

_____

_____

_____

B-5   REVIN' UP TO SETTLE DOWN

Time Required: 15 minutes
Materials Required: Markers
*This is a **doing** activity*

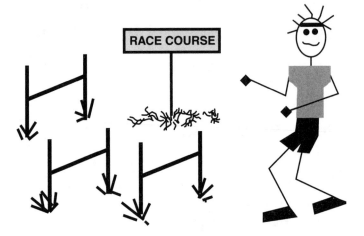

A lot of kids have trouble paying attention and getting down to business. Most of these kids love to be physical and prefer to be outside most of the time.

If you're one of these kids, you might have noticed that it's a lot easier to settle down after you've revved it up. Being physical in a smart way can burn off that extra energy and help you get down to business. Just a few minutes of good safe exercise can make all the difference!

Look at these ways to **rev it up** and think about what you'd like to do to rev it up to settle down. Give your favorite way a 1, your next favorite a 2, and your third favorite a 3. Then think of another way for you to rev up, a way that could be your own special **personal** favorite, and **draw yourself in action!**

My own special way of Revin' Up to Settle Down
Ask your helper how to plan ahead with teachers and parents, for Revin' Up! Put together a schedule for Revin' Up so you are ready when you know you will need to settle down, like just before a really long test!

Running like the wind   Jumping Jacks   Push-ups

———   ———   ———

Pull Ups ———   Jumping Rope ———   Sit-ups ———

B-6   I'D RATHER WALK

Time required: 20–30 minutes
Materials required: worksheet
*This is a **doing** activity*

Everyone gets angry sometimes. Not everyone has learned how to stop their angry feelings from getting the best of them. One way that works real well is to walk away for a few minutes from a situation that is making you mad, before losing control of your anger. We call this taking a "time-out."

Taking a time-out is a good thing and never anything to be ashamed of. Here is how it works: First, **you have to know the "anger signals"** (see B-3, Mad Me) your body gives you when you are just beginning to get angry. You can learn more about these by talking with your counselor.

Next, **you need to practice taking time-outs.** Your helper can show you how to practice so that when you really need one, it will be easy to do. It helps to remind yourself by writing "practice time-outs" or "I'd rather walk" on a sticky-note and putting it where you will see it every day, like on the inside of your bedroom door or on your bedroom mirror. **Practice taking a time-out every day for the first week and then every other day for the second week.**

When it's time for a real time-out, the important thing is to notice when your body tells you that you are beginning to get angry, and then **walking away from whatever it is that's making you mad.** It could be a friend with whom you are having a disagreement, a computer game, your homework, or just about anything. If you plan to take time-outs when a parent or teacher is making you angry, it's very important to talk to them about your time-outs ahead of time and get their permission. Spend five minutes walking in the yard, hugging your pillow, or doing something physical like push-ups, jumping jacks, or jogging. Remember to get permission from your mom and dad or teacher ahead of time. While you are taking your time-out it's best to work on calming yourself down. Your helper can give you some more ideas on how to do this. **After a few minutes you can go back and handle the problem, this time without getting angry.** Use the worksheet in your workbook to keep track of your practice and real time-outs.

Use your angry ENERGY to HELP YOURSELF by spending five minutes walking in the yard, hugging your pillow, or doing something physical like push-ups, jumping jacks, or jogging. Don't forget to get PERMISSON !

Use this worksheet to keep track of your practice and real time-outs.

Practice time-outs: (make a check for each time you practice)

First week

| MON | TUES | WED | THUR | FRI | SAT | SUN |

Second week

| MON | TUES | WED | THUR | FRI | SAT | SUN |

Real time-outs: (circle the day for the next two weeks)

MON   TUES   WED   THUR   FRI   SAT   SUN

MON   TUES   WED   THUR   FRI   SAT   SUN

<u>Talk with your helper about the time-outs you have taken!</u>

Intrapersonal Activities

C-1 TWO THINGS ABOUT ME

Time required: 20 minutes
Materials required: markers
*This is a **doing** activity*

Everybody can think of things they like about themselves and things they would like to change.

In fact, change can be good, and is a normal part of life!

If you've been told you have ADHD, you're probably told by your parents or teachers to do some things different. Things like, "stay in your seat," "hurry up with your homework," "stop interrupting," and "finish getting ready or you'll miss the bus." If you're like most kids, you get tired of being reminded, and you'd like to change at least one thing about you.

Doing things different starts with fixing Just One Thing.

With your helper, think of just one thing you want to change about yourself. Then, think of at least three things you can do to make the change.

For example, if you want to stop forgetting to get your homework in on time, you might:

1. Keep a paper calendar in the front pocket of your backpack and use it to write down every homework assignment.
2. Clean out your backpack so you can find everything you need to get the job done.
3. Ask your mom to look over your homework every night before bed time.

Use the back of the page to help <u>you</u> change Just One Thing!

My "Change One Thing" Page

One of the things I like about myself is:
(write it or draw it here)

```
┌──────────────────────────────────────────────────────────┐
│                                                          │
│                                                          │
│                                                          │
│                                                          │
│                                                          │
└──────────────────────────────────────────────────────────┘
```

The one thing I want to change about me is:

```
┌──────────────────────────────────────────────────────────┐
│                                                          │
│                                                          │
│                                                          │
│                                                          │
│                                                          │
└──────────────────────────────────────────────────────────┘
```

Three things I can do to Change One Thing about me
(write or draw them here)

1

2

3

Keep this Change One Thing page in a place you will see it, like on your bedroom mirror or on your wall.

Don't forget to practice changing Just One Thing!

C-2   I KNOW ME BEST

Time required: 10–20 minutes
Materials required: worksheet, pencil
*This is a **thinking** activity*

Everyone has a tough day now and then. And we all get down sometimes. **Kevin is a fifth grader who gets discouraged** when he has trouble with his vocabulary words, and sometimes he gets down on himself when he doesn't play basketball as well as some of the other kids.

One day Kevin talked to his mom about his feelings. Kevin learned that his mom got down sometimes too. His mom told him that she used to get discouraged a lot at her work when her boss would be in a bad mood or when her work was very busy and she couldn't keep up. She told Kevin that she doesn't get down on herself very often anymore because she learned to **encourage herself with positive thoughts.** She said to Kevin, "After all, **I know me best!**"

Here are a few of the thoughts Kevin's mom uses to "pick-herself-up" when she's having a bad day:

"I'm good at my job. I'm just having a bad day. Tomorrow will be better."

"My boss is having a bad day. He isn't really mad because of me."

"Maybe I'm not the best at some things, but I'm very good at using the computer."

What are some things Kevin can say to himself to "pick-himself-up" when he is having a tough time?

When he's having trouble with vocabulary?

_____

_____

_____

_____

_____

When he's not doing well at basketball?

_____

_____

_____

_____

_____

Do *you* know you best? List some things you're good at.

_____

_____

_____

_____

_____

_____

C-3   X MARKS THE SPOT

Time required: 15–30 minutes
Materials required: worksheet, pencil, markers
*This is a **feeling** activity*

Our feelings are a normal part of who we are. The better we understand our feelings, the better we are at managing our behavior and our lives. **Think about how you would feel in each of the following situations, and decide what to call that feeling** (or feelings, if you think of more than one; happy, sad, scared, mad, excited, proud, disgusted or some other). Then, think about **where you might feel that feeling in your body,** and show that place by placing an X on Bonnie. Next to the X **write down how your body might feel.**

My X   My Body Feels Like . . .

You are riding in a car
and you know there is
an accident up ahead

_____

You have been waiting
a long time to be picked
up after school

_____

You know there is a
great present on the
way from your
grandparents

_____

You learn your best
friend is moving away

_____

Everyone did well on the
big test except you

_____

You score the winning
points for your team

_____

Talk about your answers with your helper.

C-4 TOM TAKES HIS TEMP

Time required: 20–30 minutes
Materials required: worksheet, markers, drawing paper
*This is a **feeling** activity*

Tom learned to take his temperature from his uncle, not with a thermometer that goes under his tongue, but by using a special thermometer. This one isn't for finding out if Tom is sick. **It's used to measure his cool!**

Tom had a tough day that started when he overslept and missed the bus. Then after his mom dropped him off at school, he realized that in the rush he had forgotten his math homework. Later that day, Tom was given a hard time by his teammates for missing some shots in the basketball game. By the end of the day, Tom was <u>hot</u> and ended up in the principal's office. The next day, Tom and his uncle drew a thermometer so Tom could **measure his cool**. Tom's thermometer is below. Notice how Tom went from waking up cool, then losing his cool little by little until he was boiling! **By drawing the thermometer, Tom was then better able to pay attention to his cool slipping away, and he was eager to learn how to stop it.**

Teased by teammates.
Feel hot all over!
Can't think straight!
Want to explode!

Discovered homework was left at home.
Feel sick to stomach,
Think I can't do anything right!
Want to run away and hide!

Missed the bus!
Heart pounding, teeth clenched.
Hoping day gets better.
Want to get to school on time!

See the clock. I'm late!
Heartbeat speeds up!
Can't believe I overslept!
Wish I could go back to sleep!

Wake up cool

Make a thermometer like Tom's and use it to measure your cool!
Write down or draw the things that make your temperature rise.

Tom Takes His Temp

Make a thermometer like Tom's and use it to measure your cool!
Write down or draw the things that make your temperature rise.

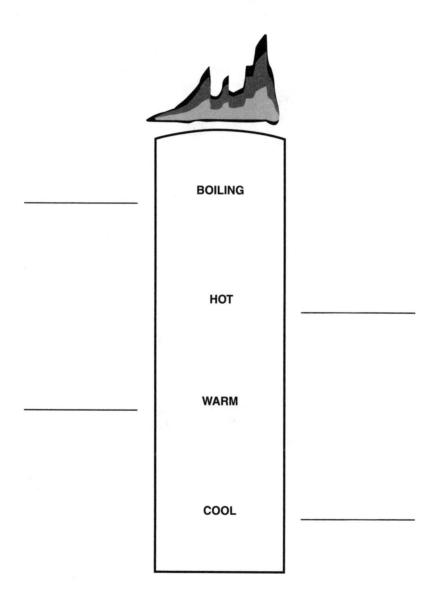

C-5 PETE TAKES THE HEAT

Time required: 10–20 minutes
Materials required: worksheet, pencil
*This is a **doing** activity*

Pete lives with his best friend Alex, who is eleven years old, in a very nice house with a big backyard and lots of green grass on which to play and chase balls. Pete used to be sad because Alex was mean to him. But Pete couldn't be any happier now. **Let's hear Pete's story.**

Hi! My name is Pete and I am a happy dog! I wasn't happy before because the people in my house were always yelling at each other. My best friend Alex is the littlest human in the house. It only figured that when bigger people were mean to Alex, he would be mean to me.

Alex finally got some help to learn how to deal with his angry feelings. He learned that everyone gets angry, **but it's not okay to take those feelings out on other people** . . . or me!

Alex learned how to change some of his thinking and some of his behavior. Learning these things, and practicing them, helped Alex feel better. Now Alex treats me like his best friend, which of course . . . I am.

I remember one time when Alex's mom yelled at him for spilling his milk at the table. When the yelling started I went under the bed. I hate yelling! Alex felt so bad about the yelling that he started yelling back at his mom, and so he got grounded and sent to his room. When Alex came into his room he was so mad he slammed his door, then threw his new model airplane against the wall. I was so scared I was shaking, and I stayed under the bed for a long time.

Now when Alex gets mad he doesn't yell or scream. He doesn't slam doors or throw things, and I don't have to be scared anymore. Look at the list of things Alex learned to do to keep from losing his cool.

Circle the things you do that keep you from LOSING YOUR COOL.

Put a star by the ones you haven't tried but would like to learn more about.

Time-out   Tense and Relax Muscles

Deep Breaths   Counting to Calm

Picture Your Relaxing Place   Hug Your Pillow

Have a Talk with Yourself

Do you have any other ways to help KEEP YOUR COOL?

_____

_____

_____

_____

Do you have someone at home like me?

_____

_____

_____

_____

Discuss your answers with your helper. He or she will want to hear about the ways you try to keep your cool, and to help you learn like Alex did.

C-6 THOUGHTS IN A BOX

Time required: 10–20 minutes
Materials required: a small cardboard
   box with lid, paper,
   marker or pencil, scissors
*This is a **doing** activity*

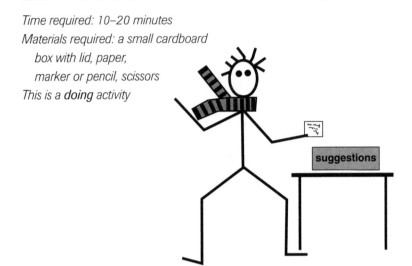

You have probably been inside a store, restaurant, or other business and have noticed a box that is labeled **"suggestions."** Anyone is allowed to write down a good idea on a piece of paper and place it in the box. The owner of the business will read the ideas and use them to make his business better. The more ideas we have to choose from, the better for solving problems. It is very important for us to have ideas for staying cool when things begin to heat up.

Find a small box, probably cardboard is best, with a lid. A shoebox works really well. Cut a slot about three inches long in the top of the box. Be sure and ask for help from your helper if you need it. **Use a big marker to print the words "suggestion box"** on the sides of your box. You can also draw on your box and make it look any way you want. **Take the box to your helper.**

Then cut out the rectangles in both workbook pages. Give half the pieces to your helper and keep half for yourself. **Think for a few minutes about the different things you can do to calm yourself** when you begin to get angry, before you lose your cool. Print or draw one idea on each piece of paper and ask your helper to put his or her ideas on the other six pieces. Each of you can fold up your ideas and place them into the box without showing them to one another.

Shake up the box and take off the lid. Take turns picking ideas from the box. Read the idea out loud and talk about it with your helper. Do this until all the ideas have been picked.

Keep your box of ideas in a place where you will see it every day. **You can use your suggestion box anytime you need it!**

Write your ideas in the boxes below then cut them out to put in the SUGGESTION BOX you will make.

Musical-Rhythmic Activities

D-1 THE RELAXATION RAP

Time required: 15–30 minutes
Materials required: worksheet, marker or pencil
*This is a **thinking** activity*

If you really like music you probably have a favorite singer or group, and a favorite song. You might even go through your day with a song in your head. Or, maybe you like to make words rhyme. Maybe rhythms or sounds are enjoyable to you. If so, **you can use this appreciation for things musical to keep your cool when things heat up.** Here is a way to get started.

Complete the phrases by drawing a line between them, so that the phrases rhyme and make sense to you. Once you have finished, **talk with your helper about which phrases you can memorize to help you stay cool.**

1. Gonna be cool . . .

2. Don't need to fret . . .

3. Not gonna yell . . .

4. Wanna have a good day . . .

5. Feeling like a bomb . . .

a. so I'm gonna "count to calm"

b. 'cus my case I can't sell

c. so I'm gonna walk away

d. 'cus cool's my best bet

e. 'cus I ain't no fool

These rap lyrics will help you to stay cool when things start to heat up. **Learn your "body signals"** so you will know when to begin repeating these rhymes in your head. Cool!

See if you can make up other lyrics to use when you think that you may lose your cool.

D-2   RADICAL RHYME FOR FEELING FINE

Time required: as needed
Materials required: worksheet, writing paper, pencil or marker
*This is a **thinking** activity*

Jenny loved to write poems. She learned from her dad that writing about feelings and how to deal with them is a very good way of learning about herself. Her dad taught Jenny a clever way to get started on writing a poem. She put a word in a middle circle with other circles around it that read "looks like," "feels like," "tastes like," "smells like," and "sounds like." Then Jenny filled in the surrounding circles. When she finished it looked like this:

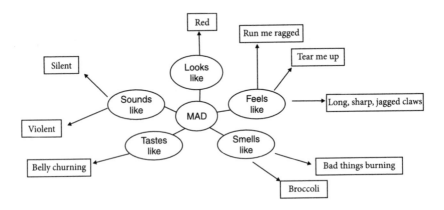

When she finished, Jenny used her ideas to write:

It sneaks up on us ever silent, then turns the day from calm to violent.

With long sharp claws both long and jagged, to tear me up and run me ragged,

Like broccoli cooking, bad things burning, its smell can leave my belly churning.

It's hard to think, I just see red, I wish I would have stayed in bed.

Complete this **Radical Rhyme for Feeling Fine** by filling in the squares. One is done for you to help you get started. After you have finished filling in the boxes, see if you can create a poem that describes what CALM means to you.

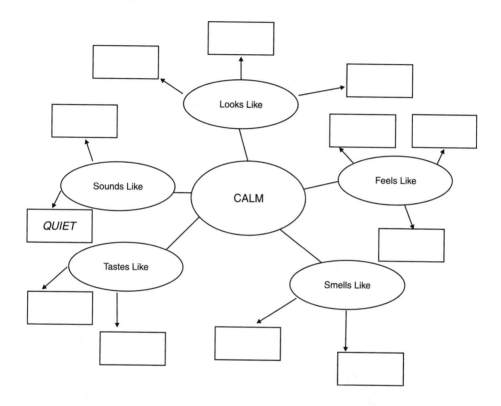

Remember your Radical Rhyme for Feeling Fine . . .

Repeat it whenever you need it!

D-3   TUNE IN TO TONE DOWN

Time required: 10–20 minutes
Materials required: worksheet, pencil or markers
*This is a **feeling** activity*

Music has special powers to grab our attention and even change our mood. Listening to your favorite tunes can cheer you up when you are feeling down, or give you energy when you are feeling lazy. **Your favorite music can even calm you down when you feel yourself getting angry.**

Lizzy and her counselor made a short list of her favorite singers and her favorite songs, then talked about how to use this music to help cheer her up, give her energy, and maybe most importantly, **to keep her cool. What are your favorite kinds of music?**

_____

_____

_____

_____

_____

_____

To make a list like Lizzy, think about your favorite music and fill-in the blanks below.

Some songs I listen to at home that cheer me up are:

_____

and

_____

Some songs I listen to that give me energy are

_____

and

_____

Some songs I think might help me stay cool or calm myself down are

_____

and

_____

What do you like about your favorite music?

_____

_____

_____

_____

Talk with your helper about how to use your favorite music to cheer up, have more energy, and **keep your cool!**

D-4 LISTENING FOR YOUR FEELINGS

Time required: 20–30 minutes
Materials required: worksheet, pencil or markers
*This is a **feeling** activity*

Have you ever noticed how a song on the radio can make us feel happy or kind of sad? Or maybe a song will make us feel like singing along or tapping our foot. Has the siren from an ambulance ever caused your heart to speed up? Maybe the whining of a newborn puppy has made you feel kind of warm and fuzzy inside. The sounds around us can affect the way we feel.

Close your eyes and imagine hearing each of the sounds listed. Pay attention to how each of the sounds makes you feel.

Draw a line from the sound to the word which best describes the feeling. If none of the feelings fit, make up one or more of your own. Draw as many lines as you need.

The clap of thunder	Sad
A swarm of bees	Mad
A babbling brook	Happy
A raging river	Disgusted
The school bus engine	Scared
A crackling fire	Surprised
The howling wind	_____
Falling rain	_____
Noisy traffic	_____
A kitten purring	_____

Think of another sound that best describes each of the feelings below:

Happiness _____

Anger _____

Fear _____

Sadness _____

Disgust _____

Surprise _____

What's your favorite sound of all? _____

_____

_____

_____

D-5 LISTENING LIKE LINDA

Time required: 15 minutes
Materials required: paper, pencil
*This is a **doing** activity*

Linda lives in a very noisy house. There is always a lot of loud chatter, the television is usually on, and sometimes Linda's family yells when they really should be talking.

Linda has gotten into the habit of **"tuning out"** a lot of the noise so that she doesn't feel like she is losing her mind!

Linda and her helper figured out that Linda was getting in trouble sometimes because she was hearing but not really **listening.** Linda had gotten so good at tuning out the noise that she was also tuning out some of the important stuff, like her **teacher's instructions, her parent's requests, and her friends' conversations.** So Linda's helper showed Linda how to learn to listen again, and some new ways to deal with the noise at home.

If you want to learn to listen like Linda, follow these steps: First, make a quick list by using pictures or words of the sounds you hear around you. After you finish, put down your paper and pencil, **take a few deep breaths, and relax your body.**

Now close your eyes for at least two minutes and really listen. . . . Begin writing down everything you didn't hear before. Can you hear background noise? How about air conditioning or machinery humming? Can you hear distant traffic or a clock ticking? How about the sounds of your own body? Can you hear your food digesting? Your heart beating? How about the soft sound of your own breathing? Now make a list of everything you didn't hear before.

If you are like Linda, you just learned that there is more to listening than just using your ears. Linda learned that being relaxed and paying attention can make hearing into something even better . . . **Listening!**

First, make a **quick list** by using pictures or words of the sounds you hear around you.

Write here   Draw here

_____

_____

_____

_____

_____

Now close your eyes for at least two minutes and really listen.
Begin writing down (and/or drawing) everything you didn't hear before.

Write here   Draw here

_____

_____

_____

_____

_____

Ask your helper to help you Listen Like Linda!

D-6 KEEPING THE BEAT

Time required: 15–30 minutes
Materials required: worksheet, drum, drumstick
*   or other materials to make the instrument*
*This is a **doing** activity*

Native Americans have understood the special powers of drumming for thousands of years, and use the rhythm of drums for many things. Nikki learned about drumming from her grandfather. He told her that making a rhythm and repeating it over and over could be like giving her soul a voice. Her grandfather told her that the rhythm could heal her pain and calm her spirit. **Then he taught her about drumming away anger.**

Nikki's grandfather gave Nikki a drum and a stick. He had covered the end of the stick with leather and secured it with a rubber band.

Next, Nikki's grandfather showed Nikki how to feel the pulse on her wrist and explained that this was the rhythm of her heart. He told Nikki to feel the rhythm of her heart a few times a day, so that she would remember its feel and pace.

Then Nikki's grandfather told her that when she gets mad or excited, her heartbeat speeds up. He explained that when this begins to happen, that Nikki can go to her room and use her drum. He told Nikki to make a rhythm that is the same pace as her relaxed heartbeat, and concentrate on the rhythm of her drum.

Nikki began to practice with her drum, and at times when she felt angry she would go to her room and begin a rhythm on her drum. Nikki learned that within minutes she could feel calm and relaxed.

Make a list of (or draw) some things that make your heartbeat speed up because you get angry.

_____

_____

_____

_____

Make a drum for yourself or ask your helper to help you. Begin practicing your drumming either with your helper or alone. Don't forget to

Give your soul a voice!

Each time you practice matching the drumbeat to your relaxed heartbeat, circle a heart.

Each time you use your drum to calm yourself down, circle a drum.

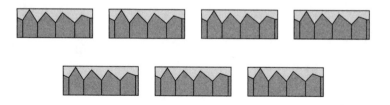

Tell your helper if you want some help to Keep the Beat!

Visual-Spatial Activities

E-1   THINK IT OR FEEL IT?

Time required: 10–20 minutes
Materials required: worksheet, pencil
*This is a **thinking** activity*

Can you tell the difference between thoughts and feelings? Test your knowledge by reading about Darcy, and then follow the instructions below.

Darcy is a sixth grader who lives with her mom and stepfather, Mac. Darcy loves to play the flute and has taken music lessons for two years. Now it's time for her big recital. A recital is when a music student gets all dressed up and plays their instrument for lots of people whom the student gets to invite. But Darcy has just learned that her stepfather will be away on a business trip on Saturday, and won't be attending the recital.

Listed below are some of the thoughts and feelings Darcy **might** be having.

If you think the sentence is a thought, circle a "thought cloud" to the right. If you think it's a feeling, then circle a heart ♡ .

Good Luck!

I wish Mac would come to see me play.

I am proud to be playing in the recital.

I am nervous about playing in front of
   so many people.

Mac likes his job more than he likes me.

I'm angry at Mac for not coming to my recital.

I know Mac is proud of me. So I guess his trip must
   be really important.

**What do you suppose you would be thinking and feeling
if you were Darcy?**

_____

_____

_____

_____

_____

_____

_____

E-2 DANIEL AND "TANTRUM"

Time required: 30–50 minutes
Materials required: worksheet, large sheet of paper,
    pencil, colored markers
*This is a **thinking** activity*

Daniel sometimes becomes so angry that he does bad things and gets in trouble. He became so discouraged that he began to think of himself as one big problem! Daniel's counselor helped him to understand that **Daniel and his problem with losing control of his anger were two very different things.**

They started by giving the problem a name; they called it "tantrum." Tantrum, Daniel began to realize, would sneak up on him when he least expected it, and grab hold of Daniel. Daniel learned that it was up to him to watch out for tantrum, and he learned ways to keep tantrum away.

Daniel drew a picture of tantrum and it looked like this:

Then Daniel drew a picture of himself when tantrum is nowhere around and it looked like this:

Daniel's problem: <u>TANTRUM!</u>   Daniel's problem is nowhere around!

Think up a name for the problem of losing control of anger that you sometimes have. _____ (fill in the blank)

Below, draw a picture of the problem you named. _____
(fill in the blank)

On a separate sheet of paper, draw a picture of yourself when _____
_____ (fill in the blank) is **nowhere around!**

E-3 NAME IT AND TAME IT

Time required: 30–50 minutes
Materials required: worksheet, pencil, workbook page or
poster-size paper, colored markers, pencils, paint.
*This is a **feeling** activity*

Anger visits us all from time to time. Sometimes that visitor creeps up on us before we know it. If we are not careful, we might lose our cool and the visitor can get the best of us.

It might help to know what the visitor looks like so that it has a harder time sneaking up without being noticed.

Take a minute and think about what it feels like when you are visited by anger. **Think about how you feel when you begin to lose your cool.** Now think about what that visitor might look like. Think about its **shape, its color(s), and its size.**

Now it's time to **give the visitor a name.** Sometimes our visitor feels like it should have a silly name, sometimes a scary name. Sometimes it feels like it should have a regular old name like Sam or Mary. Write down the name of your visitor:

_____ .

You might ask your helper to make a few copies of your picture. You can even hang one in your bedroom to remind you to keep an eye out.

You might also want to wad up one of the pictures into a ball and use it for shooting some hoops. Maybe you and your helper can shoot some hoops, using the wastebasket in the room. Playing with your visitor can help you to see that it is not so scary after all. **Our visitor is just another part of ourselves that we need to get to know, make peace with, and manage!**

Now, **draw a picture of the visitor.** Take your time and really use your imagination to make your picture look like the feeling you remember.

Close your eyes and create a picture of your visitor in your mind . . .

When you are finished drawing your picture, discuss it with your helper.

My visitor's name is _____ .

E-4   TIM TOES THE LINE

Time required: 20–40 minutes
Materials required: worksheet, pencil, drawing paper, markers
*This is a **feeling** activity*

Tim loved to draw so his helper showed Tim how to use his talent to learn about his feelings and keep his cool.

One day on the playground, Tim was talking with his friend when a soccer ball hit him in the head. The ball surprised Tim but he wasn't really hurt. Tim got very mad and thought that his classmate Bryan had hit Tim with the ball on purpose. **Tim didn't stop to think.**

Tim's helper asked Tim to draw about what happened on a "timeline." A timeline is for remembering things in the order in which they happened. When Tim drew his timeline it looked like this:

Then his helper asked Tim to draw another timeline. Tim drew what might have happened if he had **stopped, relaxed, and thought** before letting himself lose his temper. The new timeline looked like this (helper: show timeline to child, discuss, and help fill in the last event):

Think of a time when you let anger get the best of you because you didn't stop, relax, and think. Remember how you felt? Draw a timeline that shows what happened.

Next, draw a timeline showing what might have happened had you stopped, relaxed, and thought. How do you suppose you would have felt?

_____

_____

_____

_____

_____

_____

E-5 PICK A PATH FOR PRINCE

Time required: 30 minutes
Materials required: marker, separate paper optional
*This is a **thinking** activity*

Prince is a two-year-old Australian Shepherd, but he just thinks of himself as a "cow dog." Prince is super at keeping the cows all together when his master is moving the cows from one pasture to another.

But today, Prince has a problem.

Prince went over a hill looking for strays and when he came back, his master and the herd were gone. Now, Prince has to figure out how to get all the way home.

Prince is a very smart dog but he's never had to try and find his way home from a long way away.

In fact, on his journey home, Prince will come across lots of dangers. When he does, and if he can figure out the best thing to do, he can look back on this day as a thrilling adventure.

Prince has nearly 10 miles to cover in 100-degree heat, across rocky hills with only a few scattered trees. There's a river a few miles ahead, and no other water around.

On the next page, see if you can match up the *challenges* Prince is facing, with the *strategies* he could use to eventually make it home. There might be more than one strategy for one challenge.

Draw a line from the challenge to the strateg(ies) that will help Prince make it home.

Pick a Path for Prince

Challenges

1. 100-degree heat!

2. No water nearby!

3. A pack of mean coyotes!

4. A deep and rushing river!

Strategies

a. Climb a hill and look around

b. Look for a bridge or a shallow spot

c. Travel after the sun goes behind a hill

d. Rest under a tree in the afternoon

e. Take a good long drink from the river

With your helper, draw a map of Prince's journey home, showing the pasture where he started, the hills, the river, the coyotes, and his home. Write down or draw the strategies Prince uses to overcome the challenges and make his way home.

E-6   FILLING IN THE GAPS

Time required: 20 minutes
Materials required: paper, markers
*This is a **doing** activity*

This is a sort of puzzle for learning about what might happen 'if.'

Read the story, and then look at the 'ifs.' Think for a moment about your answers. Then on the next page, use that creative imagination to draw what might happen 'if,' and what you would do to make things right again. **Have a great time filling in the gaps!**

Will and Daisy are sixth graders. Having gotten their parents permission the night before, Will and Daisy leave school one afternoon after the bell, and head for the video arcade a few blocks away. They expected that after the 20-minute walk, they would have about half an hour to play video games. Then Daisy had an idea. She suggested that instead of sticking to the sidewalk, they cut through the woods, and save an extra ten minutes for games.

Neither Daisy nor Will had ever been through those woods before, so they didn't know what they might find. But having more time to play sure sounded good, so off they went. While deep in the woods, what might happen 'if,' and what would you do about it?

What if . . . huge dark clouds suddenly appear overhead, and a vicious thunderstorm begins?

What if . . . Will and Daisy come upon a giant spider web between two trees along their path, with a giant furry spider right in the center?

What if . . . the path suddenly splits in two, and neither Will nor Daisy know which one leads back to civilization?

What if . . . they come upon a man they've never seen before, and he asks if they want to ride along on his motorbike?

Discuss all the 'what ifs' with your helper.

Interpersonal Activities

F-1 PECKING ORDER

Time required: 20–30 minutes
Materials required: worksheet, markers or pencil
*This is a **thinking** activity*

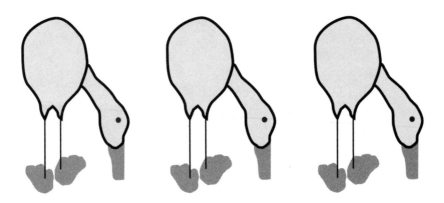

In the life of a child who is having trouble with anger, there are usually others close to the child who also have trouble with anger. Often, the anger gets passed from the biggest or strongest to someone not as big. That person then passes it to another who is not as big as him, and so on, like an unwanted toy that is just taking up space. **Sometimes, when someone who has trouble with anger picks on us, we, in turn, pick on someone smaller than we are.** Maybe it's a friend, a little brother or sister, or maybe even our dog or cat.

Can you name the ducks on the "pecking line" below, starting with the strongest or biggest and finishing with the smallest or weakest (they may be people in your life who pass on anger)?

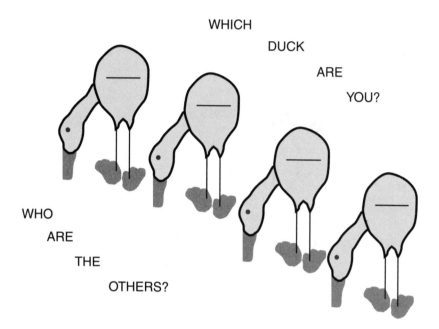

WHICH

DUCK

ARE

YOU?

WHO

ARE

THE

OTHERS?

What can <u>you</u> do to stop this from going on and on? (discuss with your helper)

_____

_____

_____

_____

_____

_____

_____

F–2   COOL LIKE WHO?

Time required: 20–30 minutes
Materials required: worksheet, pencil or markers
*This is a **thinking** activity*

Think of an adult in your life who knows how to **be cool**. This person can stay calm even when things heat up. This person might be a teacher, or a relative like an uncle or older brother. If you have trouble thinking of someone you know, then think of someone on TV or the movies. Remember, this person seems to know how to keep his or her cool no matter what. Got him in mind?

What's his name? _____

Maybe you can learn some things from this cool person. Ready to try? Here we go. . . .

Let's pretend this cool person has a really tough day, the kind of day we all have now and then, when everything seems to go wrong. **How do you think this cool person gets through a day like this, without losing his or her cool?**

What if

(circle a, b, c, or write in another answer)

1. His alarm clock doesn't go off on the first day of his new job at the video store. He's going to be late.
   Would he:

   a. roll over and go back to sleep
   b. throw the clock across his bedroom and leave a hole in the wall
   c. get to work and ask his boss if he can work late to make up the time
   d. _____

2. His first customer yells at him because the movie the customer wants is not in.
   Would he:

   a. yell back at the customer and challenge him to a fight
   b. tell the customer that the problem is beyond his control and offer to call the customer when the movie comes in
   c. tell his boss he's had enough of this stinking job
   d. _____

3. Let's suppose this cool guy gets home and finds his dog has chewed up his favorite shoes.
   What are some things he might do to keep from losing his cool?

   a. _____
   b. _____
   c. _____

Your helper can help you to learn more from this cool person about how to handle problems and keep your cool without losing control.

F-3   FRIENDS OR FOES?

Time required: 15–20 minutes
Materials required: worksheet, pencil or marker
*This is a **feeling** activity*

Sara and Tina were best friends. One day at school, Tina chose the new girl at school to be her partner for the science project. After school, Sara blocked the hallway and challenged Tina to a fight.

What do you think Sara was **feeling**?

_____

_____

_____

_____

What do you think Sara was **thinking**?

_____

_____

_____

_____

What are some better ways that Sara can deal with her feelings without challenging Tina to a fight?

_____

_____

_____

_____

_____

_____

When did you last have the same feelings and thoughts as Sara and what did you do?

_____

_____

_____

_____

_____

_____

F–4   I KNOW THAT FACE

Time required: 10–20 minutes
Materials required: worksheet, marker or pencil
*This is a **feeling** activity*

Did you know that there are only six different feelings that can be expressed by making a face and that these are understood in every country in the world?

Can you name the feelings on the faces of the six kids below?

_____   _____   _____

_____   _____   _____

What do you think might be happening to the person in each of these pictures?

_____

_____

_____

_____

_____

_____

_____

F-5 SIGN ON THE LINE

Time required: 10–15 minutes
Materials required: worksheet, pencil or marker
*This is a **doing** activity*

People make contracts when they are willing to do something in return for something from someone else. A contract is an agreement between people. When someone buys a car they usually sign a contract that says that they agree to pay the seller a specific amount of money and in return the seller agrees to hand over the car.

Contracts are sometimes used to help kids manage their angry feelings. You and your helper can use the contract below to help you remember to use the things you have been learning about keeping your cool.

Here's how it works. Your helper will ask you to **remember to use a number of skills during the week,** such as deep breathing, taking a time-out, being assertive, or any of the others. In return for using these skills, your **helper agrees to do something with you that you might like,** such as playing a favorite computer game, taking a walk, or going for ice cream.

A contract might serve as a good reminder if you put it in a place where you will see it often during the week. You could put it on your bedroom mirror or on your refrigerator door.

Fill in the contract below with your helper, and use the other contract when you need it by filling it in.

CONTRACT

I, _____ agree to use the following skills for the next week,

to help manage my angry feelings: _____

and in return, my helper _____ agrees to

_____ with me.

Signed _____ Date _____

Helper _____

CONTRACT

_____

_____

_____

_____

_____

_____

_____   _____

F-6 LEARNING ANOTHER LANGUAGE

Time required: 20–30 minutes
Materials required: worksheet
*This is a **doing** activity*

Most of what we say to other people is not spoken with words but by the way we use our bodies. This is called "body language." Our bodies can tell others what we are feeling even without saying a word. Also, if we know body language, we can learn what others may be feeling just by watching how they are using their bodies.

Here is a game you can play with your helper to help you learn about body language. Together with your helper, **look at the pictures on the next page and guess what these people are feeling. Talk with your helper about your answers.**

What are these people feeling?

_____   _____   _____   _____

_____   _____   _____   _____

_____   _____   _____   _____

_____   _____   _____   _____

Next, your helper is going to give you three different sets of body language. Can you guess how he or she is pretending to feel?

Now it's your turn. **Show your helper three different sets of body language and see if he or she can guess what you are feeling.** If you want some help, here are some ideas:

1. You are looking nervous about a test you have to take,

2. You are feeling angry because you are being picked on by a classmate, and

3. You are feeling excited about playing a new video game.

How might learning about body language help you in your everyday life?

WORKBOOK G

Verbal-Linguistic Activities

G-1   BLACK-AND-WHITE BELINDA

Time required: 20–30 minutes
Materials required: worksheet, markers or pencil
*This is a **thinking** activity*

Ever wonder what the world would look like if there were only black and white? The sky would not be bright blue, the forest would lose its beautiful deep green, and the sunset would have none of its splendor at all. **Wouldn't our lives be dull without color? And wouldn't it be harder to tell one thing from another?**

Belinda could see the colors around her okay, but inside her head there was only black and white. If she did poorly on her test she could only think that she was dumb. If her mother punished her for being late she could only think that her mother didn't love her. And if her best friend asked someone else to spend the night then Belinda was sure that she had lost her best friend. She was given the nickname "Black and White Belinda."

Do you think in black and white or do you see the different beautiful colors inside your head?

Read each of these situations and then circle the best thought that goes with it. Beware of thinking like Black and White Belinda!

1. You get back a math quiz and see that you circled the wrong answer to an easy problem.

    a. I will never be any good at math.

    b. I wasn't paying attention and will do better next time.

2. Your mom decides you can't stay over at your friend's house on a school night.

    a. I wish I could go but my mom wants me to not be tired at school.

    b. I never get to have any fun!

3. You miss the last shot of the game and your team loses.

    a. I am a terrible athlete and everyone hates me.

    b. I tried my best. No one makes every shot.

4. Your dad often comes home late at night and you hardly get to see him.

    a. I wish Dad would spend more time with me. He works so hard for us.

    b. My dad likes his job more than me.

G-2   THE MIGHTY THINKING OAK

Time required: 20–40 minutes
Materials required: worksheet, pencil or markers, drawing paper
*This is a **thinking** activity*

The things we think lead to other thoughts much the same way that the branch of the oak tree starts at the trunk and leads to a bunch of smaller branches. These smaller branches finally lead to the fresh green leaves, **much like our thoughts lead to our actions.**

Sara loved the mountains, the clean cool air, the calm blue lake, and especially the giant trees. Her favorite tree was the mighty oak. Sara could sit beneath an oak for hours and think of all the good things about her life. The mighty oak was strong and green, and it gave cool shade on even the hottest day. Sara couldn't wait to see her favorite tree again! Sara and her helper made a drawing that showed how Sara's thinking helped her to deal with a big disappointment in her life, when **Sara got the measles and missed out on going to summer camp with** her best friend, Julie.

When she was well enough, she told her mom about her favorite tree and what it meant to her. And Sara told her mom all about feeling sad and mad when she missed the trip. Sara's mom was very proud of her for how she handled her feelings, and together they drew a picture of **Sara's Mighty Thinking Oak!**

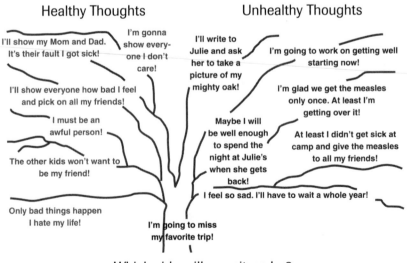

Healthy Thoughts   Unhealthy Thoughts

I'll show my Mom and Dad. It's their fault I got sick!

I'm gonna show everyone I don't care!

I'll write to Julie and ask her to take a picture of my mighty oak!

I'm going to work on getting well starting now!

I'll show everyone how bad I feel and pick on all my friends!

I must be an awful person!

I'm glad we get the measles only once. At least I'm getting over it!

The other kids won't want to be my friend!

Maybe I will be well enough to spend the night at Julie's when she gets back!

At least I didn't get sick at camp and give the measles to all my friends!

I feel so sad. I'll have to wait a whole year!

Only bad things happen I hate my life!

I'm going to miss my favorite trip!

Which side will you sit under?

Draw a picture of your own <u>Mighty Thinking Oak!</u>

G-3   PUZZLED BY YOUR FEELINGS?

Time required: 30–50 minutes
Materials needed: worksheet, pencil or marker
*This is a **feeling** activity*

Sam and Pete are good friends. Then one day at school Sam calls Pete a "big baby" because Pete complained to a teacher when a bigger boy wouldn't stop picking on him. Can you think of how this might have made Pete feel?

Solving the crossword puzzle will give you some possible answers. Be sure to discuss your answers with your helper, and ask for help if you need it.

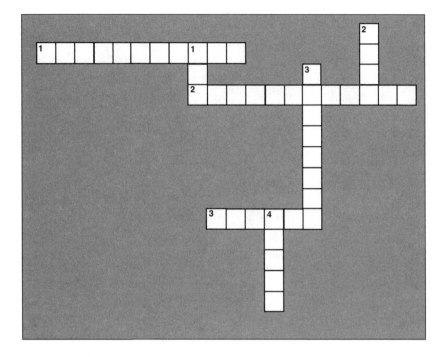

Across:

1. self-conscious or ashamed
2. frustrated or let down
3. scared

Down:

1. sorrowful
2. wounded
3. unsure
4. mad

How Would You Feel?

_____

_____

_____

_____

_____

G-4   UNSCRAMBLE YOUR FEELINGS

Time required: 20–40 minutes
Materials needed: worksheet, markers or pencil, scratch paper
*This is a **feeling** activity*

Feelings are something we all have. Some feelings are comfortable, like when we feel **happy, excited, or loved**. Some feelings, like **sad, hurt, or scared**, are not so comfortable. **Feelings are just feelings and they can't really hurt us.** Once we understand our feelings, we are better able to express them in a healthy way. When we are happy, we smile and laugh. When we are sad, we might cry. If we are confused, we say so and ask for help. These are all healthy ways of express-ing what we feel. **If we don't know what we feel, we have trouble expressing our feelings in a healthy way.** This sometimes leads to trouble.

Chris worked very hard on his science project that was about volcanoes. He was proud of his work and was eager to show it to his teacher and classmates. Chris set the volcano on the empty bus seat behind him for the ride to school, then forgot about it when he arrived. When Chris's teacher asked Chris to turn in his project he realized he had left the volcano on the bus.

Think about what Chris might be feeling. Have fun unscrambling the letters to spell out the feelings that go along with the face next to each word. These are only some of many possible feelings. As always, discuss each solved puzzle with your helper.

DARSSMEEBRA

 ADS

IWRRODE

 TRESFRUDAT

G-5 WHEN ANGER BEGINS

Time required: 30–40 minutes
Materials required: worksheet, pencil or marker
*This is a **doing** activity*

There are many things we can do when we first start to feel angry to stop the anger from growing and getting the better of us. Start by writing down some of your ideas for stopping angry behavior in its tracks!

Solving the puzzle below will give you some helpful ideas about what you can do when you begin to feel angry. It's important to talk with your helper about knowing your "angry signals," so that you know when to use the answers below.

Across:

1. To get physical and burn off energy
2. To go somewhere else for a few minutes, where you can get calm
3. Use humor

Down:

1. You use numbers to do this
2. You use your feet for this
3. Filling up on air
4. To do this you have to hold something soft and squishy

Talk to your helper about practicing these ways of keeping cool.

G-6   LARRY LEARNS TO LISTEN

Time required: 10–20 minutes
Materials required: worksheet
*This is a **doing** activity*

Larry is a sixth grader who has a best friend named Daniel. Larry and Daniel were not always best friends. In fact, they fought a lot. Larry says they fought because Daniel always said mean things to him. But then a funny thing happened. **Larry learned to Listen!**

Larry learned to **check out** what Daniel was saying to him, and **what do you think happened?** Larry found out that Daniel wasn't being mean, he just had a little trouble saying what he meant.

To show you how it went, look below. Look at what Daniel **said**, what Larry "heard," and what Daniel **meant**.

Daniel said:	"I won't be going to the game with you and your dad. I have other things to do."
Larry heard:	"I don't want to go to the dumb game with you. I have better things to do."
What Daniel meant:	"I can't go to the game with you. I wish I could but I got grounded."

Daniel said: "I'm going to sit with Tina on the bus today."

Larry heard: "I don't want to sit with you on the bus anymore."

What Daniel meant: "Tina and I have to study our spelling words on the way to school or I'm in big trouble."

Larry learned to check out what Daniel was saying before guessing. He did this by asking certain questions in a nice way. These questions usually start with phrases like "**do you mean**" or "**so then**" or "**is that because.**"

Did you ever think you knew what someone meant and later found out it wasn't what they meant at all? What happened?

_____

_____

_____

_____

_____

_____

What can you say to find out what someone means if you're not sure?

_____

_____

_____

_____

_____

_____

Ask your helper to help you practice. Don't forget to **check it out!**

Answer Guide

Some of the interventions call for specific answers, which you will find here.

Workbook A (pages 105–119)	A-1	W. Disney . . . . Castle Galileo . . . . Telescope H. Ford . . . . Automobile R. Williams . . . . Clown/Comedian J. Lennon . . . . Musical notes

	A-4	Across 1. Ashamed 2. Proud 3. Sad 4. Scared	Down 1. Surprised 2. Glad

Workbook D (pages 147–160)	D-1	1. e 2. d 3. b 4. c 5. a

Workbook E (pages 161–174)	E-1	I wish Mac . . . ⟶ (thought bubble) I am proud . . . ⟶ (heart) I am nervous . . . ⟶ (heart) Mac likes his . . . ⟶ (thought bubble) I'm angry . . . ⟶ (heart) I know Mac is proud . . . ⟶ (thought bubble)

| Workbook F | F-2 | 1. c |
| (pages 175–188) | | 2. b |

F-4

Surprised
Sad
Mad (Angry)
Confused
Happy
Scared

F-6

1st person-mad/angry
2nd person-sad
3rd person-happy/glad
4th person-surprised

Workbook G   G-1

You get back . . . b
Your mom decides . . . a
You miss the last . . . b
Your dad often comes . . . a

(pages 189–202)

G-3

Across	Down
1. Embarassed	1. Sad
2. Disappointed	2. Hurt
3. Afraid	3. Confused
	4. Angry

G-4

1st face on right-Embarrassed
1st face on left-Sad
2nd face on right-Worried
Last face on left-Frustrated

G-5

Across	Down
1. Exercise	1. Count to Ten
2. Take Time Out	2. Walk Away
3. Laugh It Off	3. Deep Breathing
	4. Hug Your Pillow

References

References Cited

Amen, D. *Healing ADD*. New York: Berkley Books, 2001.

American Academy of Pediatrics

American Psychiatric Association. *Diagnostic and Statistical Manual of Mental Disorders DSM-IV-TR Fourth Edition*. Washington, DC: American Psychiatric Publishing, Inc., 2000.

Armstrong, T. *Seven Kinds of Smart*. New York: Plume, 1993.

Armstrong, T. *The Myth of the ADD Child: 50 Ways to Improve Your Child's Behavior and Attention Span without Drugs, Labels, or Coercion*. New York: Plume, 1997.

Bandura, A., D. Ross, and S. A. Ross. "Transmission of aggressions through imitation of aggressive models." *Journal of Abnormal and Social Psychology* 63: 572-582.

Barkley, R. *Attention-Deficit Hyperactivity Disorder*. New York: Guilford Press, 1998.

Connors, C. *Attention Deficit Hyperactivity Disorder: The Latest Assessment and Treatment Strategies*. Kansas City: Compact Clinicals, 2006.

Cozolino, L. *The Neuroscience of Psychotherapy*. New York: W.W. Norton, 2002.

Damasio, A. *Descartes' Error*. New York: Quill, 1994.

Fuller, C. *Unlocking Your Child's Learning Potential*. Colorado Springs: Pinon, 1994.

Gardner, H. *Frames of Mind: The Theory of Multiple Intelligences*. New York: Basic Books, 1983.

Gardner, H. *Multiple Intelligences: New Horizons*. New York: Basic Books, 2006.

Goldberg, E. *The Executive Brain, Frontal Lobes and the Civilized Mind.* New York: University Press, 2001.

Golden, D. "Building a Better Brain." *Life* (July 1994): 62-70.

Glasser, H. and J. Easley. *Transforming the Difficult Child.* Tucson, AZ: Nurtured Heart, 1998.

Glasser, H. *101 Reasons to Avoid Ritalin Like the Plague.* Tucson, AZ: Nurtured Heart: 2005.

Gould, E., A. J. Reeves, M. S. Graziano, and C. G. Gross. "Neurogenesis in the cortex of adult primates." *Science* 286, no. 5439 (1999): 548-552.

Hallowel, E. and J. Ratey. *Driven to Distraction.* New York: Touchstone, 1995.

Hamm, R.J., M. D. Temple, D. M. O'Dell, B. R. Pike, and B. G. Lyeth. "Exposure to environmental complexity promotes recovery of cognitive function after brain injury," *Journal of Neurotrauma* 13, no. 1 (1996): 41-47.

Harlow, J. Recovery from the passage of an iron bar through the head, *Publications of the Massachusetts Medical Society* 2:327-47, 1868, and Passage of an iron bar through the head, *Boston Medical and Surgical Journal* 39:389, 1848-49.

Hartmann, T. *ADHD Secrets of Success: Coaching Yourself to Fulfillment in the Business World.* New York: Select Books, 2002.

Kanel, K. *A Guide to Crisis Intervention* 3. Belmont, CA: Thomson Brooks/ Cole, 2006.

Lazear, D. *Multiple Intelligence Approaches to Assessment.* Tucson, AZ: Zephyr Press, 1994.

LeDoux, J. *The Synaptic Self.* New York: Viking Penguin, 2002.

Low, Keith. Famous People with Attention Deficit Disorder. About.com: ADD, 2007. http://add.about.com/od/famouspeoplewithadhd/a/famouspeople .htm.

Lubar, J. *Quantitative Electrocephalographic Analysis (QEEG) Databases for Neurotherapy: Description, Validation, and Application.* New York: Hayworth Medical Press, 2003.

MarketWatch. "Caffeine Content on Soda Labels." *Wall Street Journal,* February 27, 2007.

Neurological basis for ADHD, A. Singer, E. *Technology Review* (August 9, 2007). http://www.technologyreview.com/Biotech/19197/

Perry, B. "Helping Traumatized Children." The Child Trauma Academy, 1999. www.childtrauma.org.

Perry, B. "Aggression and Violence: The Neurobiology of Experience." Scholastic, 2007. http://teacher.scholastic.com.

Thomas, K. "Stealing and Dealing Ritalin," *USA Today*, November 27, 2000.

Recommended Reading

Amen, D. *Change Your Brain Change Your Life.* New York: Three Rivers Press, 1998.

"Are we giving our kids too many drugs?" Kluger, K. *Time.* October, 2003.

Bar-On, R., D. Trandel, N. Denburg, and A. Bechara. "Exploring the neurological substrate of emotional and social intelligence." *Brain: A Journal of Neurology* 126, no. 8 (August): 790-1800.

Bloom, P. "How children learn the meaning of words." *Behavioral and Brain Sciences*, 2001.

Brain age: Train your brain in minutes a day!. Nintendo. www.brainage.com/launcharticles.jsp, 2006.

Campbell, D. *The Mozart Effect.* New York: Avon, 1997.

Dalai Lama, and D. Goleman. *Destructive Emotions.* New York: Bantam Dell, 2003.

Freeman, J., D. Epston, and D. Lobovitz. *Playful Approaches to Serious Problems.* New York: W.W. Norton, 1997.

Goldstein, A., B. Glick, and J. Gibbs. *Aggression Replacement Therapy.* Champaign, IL: Research Press, 1998.

Goleman, D. *Emotional Intelligence.* New York: Bantam, 1995.

Johnson, K. *Trauma in the Lives of Children.* Alameda, CA: Hunter House, 1989.

Kemperman, G., H. G. Kuhn, and F. H. Gage. "More hippocampal neurons in adult mice living in an enriched environment." *Nature* 386, no. 6624 (1997): 493-495.

Lazear, D. *Seven Pathways of Learning.* Tucson, AZ: Zephyr Press, 1994.

LeDoux, J. "Emotions, memory, and the brain," *Scientific American* 270 (1994): 50-57.

Lockwood, K., A. Marcotte, and C. Stern. "Differentiation of attention/hyperactivity disorder subtypes: application of a neuropsychological model of attention." *Journal of Clinical and Experimental Neuropsychology* 23, no. 3 (2001):317-330.

Lou, H., L. Hendrickson, and P. Bruhn. "Focal cerebral hypoperfusion in children with dysphasia and/or attention deficit disorder." *Neurology* 41, no. 8 (1984).

"Medicating Young Minds" Kluger, J. *Time.* November, 2003.

Nadeau, K, and E. Dixon. *Learning to Slow Down and Pay Attention.* Washington, DC: Magination Press, 2005.

Neiser, U., G. Boodoo, T. Bouchard, A. Boykin, N. Brody, S. Ceci, D. Halpern, J. Loehlin, R. Perloff, and S. Urbina, S. "Intelligence: knowns and unknowns." *American Psychologist* 51 (1996):77-101.

Oppositional Defiant Disorder, Conduct Disorder, and the Role of Attachment. Eau Clair, WI: MEDS-PDN, 2007.

Perry, B. "Neurodevelopment and the neurophysiology of trauma," *The APSAC Advisor* 6, no. 1-2 (1993).

Perry, B. *Maltreated Children: Experience, Brain Development and the Next Generation.* New York: Norton, 1995.

Phelan, T. *1-2-3 Magic: Effective Discipline for Children 2-12* 3. Glen Ellyn, IL: Parents Magic, 2003.

ADHD/ADD in girls. Raibner, D. http://helpforadd.com/add-in-girls/ , 2006.

ADHD in girls. Swan, N. The Health Report. http://www.abc.net.au/rn/healthreport/stories/2007/1895618.htm

Reiff, M. *ADHD. A Complete and Authoritative Guide.* Elk Grove Village: American Academy of Pediatrics, 2004.

Saarni, C. *The Development of Emotional Competence.* New York: Guilford Press, 1999.

Salovey, P., and D. Sluyter. *Emotional Development and Emotional Intelligence.* New York: Basic Books, 1997.

Schiraldi, G. *The Anger Management Sourcebook.* Chicago: Contemporary Books, 2002.

Semmelroth, C., and D. Smith. *The Anger Habit.* Lincoln, NE: Writers Showcase, 2000.

Siegel, D. *The Developing Mind.* New York: Guilford Press, 1999.

Spackman, M. P. "How to do things with emotions.," *The Journal of Mind and Behavior* 23, no. 4 (Autumn 2002):393-412.

Wagemaker, H. *Psychiatric Medications and our Children: A Parent's Guide.* Ponte Vedra Publishing: Pontre Vedra Beach, 2003.

Watching Wrestling Positively Associated with Date Fighting, Say Researchers. American Academy of Pediatrics (2001). www.sciencedaily.com/releases/2001/05/010503092632.htm.

Wells, R.H. *Breakthrough Strategies to Teach and Counsel Troubled Kids.* Woodburn, OR: Youth Change, 1993.

Williams, E. (2007) Presenter on Disruptive, Unmotivated, Struggling, At-Risk Students. MEDS-PDN.

Index